Innovative Concepts for Alternative Migration Policies

IMISCOE (International Migration, Integration and Social Cohesion)

IMISCOE is a European Commission-funded Network of Excellence of more than 350 scientists from various research institutes that specialise in migration and integration issues in Europe. These researchers, who come from all branches of the economic and social sciences, the humanities and law, implement an integrated, multidisciplinary and internationally comparative research programme that focuses on Europe's migration and integration challenges.

Within the programme, existing research is integrated and new research lines are developed to address issues crucial to European-level policymaking and provide a theory-based design to implement new research.

The publication programme of IMISCOE is based on five distinct publication profiles, designed to make its research and results available to scientists, policymakers and the public at large. High-quality manuscripts written by – or in cooperation with – IMISCOE members are published in these five series. An editorial committee coordinates the review process of the manuscripts. The five series are:
1. Joint Studies
2. Research
3. Dissertations
4. Reports
5. Textbooks

More information on the network can be found at www.imiscoe.org.

IMISCOE **Reports** includes publications resulting from research of IMISCOE members, such as research monographs and edited volumes.

Innovative Concepts for Alternative Migration Policies

Ten Innovative Approaches to the Challenges
of Migration in the 21st Century

Michael Jandl (Ed.)
International Centre for Migration Policy Development
(ICMPD)

IMISCOE Reports

AMSTERDAM UNIVERSITY PRESS

Cover design: Studio Jan de Boer BNO, Amsterdam
Layout: Fito Prepublishing, Almere

ISBN   978 90 5356 990 0
NUR   741 / 763

Contents

Foreword

Towards the end of 2005, extensive media coverage of the tragic events in Ceuta and Melilla, where several hundred desperate but determined migrants had stormed the protective fences of these tiny Spanish exclaves to get into EU territory, reminded us once again that traditional mechanisms of migration management have run into severe trouble and that new, innovative concepts for the regulation of migration are called for. Yet, new ideas for regulating regular migration, dealing with irregular migration and providing international protection to those in need of it remain elusive and untested. While several innovative concepts have been suggested over the past few years – such as the 'People Flow' approach spearheaded by Theo Veenkamp, the 'Migration Tax' proposal by Jagdhish Baghwati or the 'Auctioning of work permits' suggested by Thomas Straubhaar – there is no serious discussion of these either at the policy level or among migration researchers.

To address this yawning gap between the daily realities of migration events, shaping the policy agendas of governments around the world – and the analytical world of migration researchers concerned with scientific description and explanation rather than prescription and advice – I decided to launch a challenge to those esteemed colleagues willing to push forward their formidable knowledge in the migration research domain into the uncharted and controversial terrain of policy innovation.

With the joint financial support of the IMISCOE Network of Excellence and the International Centre for Migration Policy Development (ICMPD), a workshop was organised and a call for papers went out with the explicit task of proposing and discussing new, alternative and innovative approaches to the management of migration. The participants invited were asked to produce brief overviews of their innovative policy concepts, which would then be subjected to close scrutiny and criticism by their colleagues and invited migration policymakers during the two-day workshop sessions.

Fortunately, the initiative was met with a strong response both from the migration research community and from migration policymakers interested in exploring innovative policy ideas away from the current mainstream. After reviewing a considerable number of abstracts, a dozen researchers were asked to elaborate their cutting-edge thinking on migration policy into innovative proposals to be discussed at the workshop. The workshop was held in Vienna in March 2006 and brought together 24 participants from academia, think tanks, international organisations and national administrations in a constructive and highly stimulating atmosphere. Using the critique and suggestions raised at the workshop, the authors were asked to revise and refine their papers once again before the full publication was submitted to the IMISCOE Editorial Committee for quality review.

Finally, the main outcomes of our pioneering exercise were a widely distributed policy brief and the longer publication in front of you. We hope that the very force of the many fresh ideas presented here will stimulate further debate and new thinking at the academic as well as the policy level. We know that the way from ideas to their implementation is a long one, but without good ideas there is simply no way.

Michael Jandl
Vienna, June 2006

Introduction and overview

Michael Jandl, ICMPD[1]

Introductory remarks

There is a growing conviction among migration researchers, policy-makers and a concerned public that current migration regimes do not produce generally desired migration outcomes. On the contrary, while policymakers wrestle with the question of how to deal with growing migration pressures and balance the present-day needs of dynamic labour markets with long-term goals of social cohesion, social security and humanitarian concerns, migration outcomes seem to be removed ever further from policy goals. To stimulate new thinking, therefore, an international workshop was convened by ICMPD in Vienna under the umbrella of the IMISCOE Network of Excellence with a special call for papers that had the explicit purpose to bring forward new, alternative and innovative approaches to the management of migration. Participants were asked to produce brief overviews of innovative policy concepts that were then subjected to close scrutiny and criticism from researchers and practitioners.

The joint ICMPD/IMISCOE workshop took place in Vienna in March 2006 with two dozen participants from academia, think tanks, international organisations and national administrations, who all engaged in a very lively yet constructive dialogue over the course of two days. It gave the authors of the innovative policy proposals presented in this volume an opportunity to contrast their cutting-edge thinking on redesigning migration policy with the needs and concerns of practitioners at the national and European levels. It also gave them an opportunity to refine and modify their policy proposals in order to give their ideas a still stronger thrust.

Structure of the book

The following sections will provide a quick overview of the contributions contained in this volume. As an overview, they are necessarily exceedingly short and cannot in any way do justice to the full force of the arguments put forward by their authors. For this, the reader has to

turn to the individual contributions of their authors. To preserve origin-
ality of thinking, the editing of all chapters has been kept to a minimum and the reader will notice that authenticity has been given preference to a common formal structure.

At the end of the single contributions, a concluding section identifies
several common themes and principles in the design of alternative migration policies that run across the ten individual proposals. Based on
the strengths of the combined ideas presented by the authors, it is here
that the would-be architect of new migration policies should find new
basic design principles for innovative policy approaches.

Following the individual chapters and the concluding chapter is a
part devoted to the ICMPD/IMISCOE Workshop on Innovative Concepts for Alternative Migration Policies that took place in March 2006
in Vienna. Written by our three conference rapporteurs, a comprehensive conference report reflects the discussions of the policy concepts as
they took place during the workshop, complete with comments, criticisms and responses of the authors. This part is completed by the
workshop programme and a list of workshop participants.

Finally, the last page provides a short biographical note on the
authors of this volume as well as their institutional affiliations with
links to their homepages.

Ten proposals for innovative migration policies

During the two-day workshop sessions a total of ten innovative policy
papers were presented and discussed.[2] These papers have been substantially revised and edited and are presented in the following chapters. In the remainder of this chapter, I will briefly discuss the main
ideas of each of these proposals.

In his presentation 'Temporary Migration Programmes: potentials,
problems and prerequisites', Jeff Crisp notes a renewed interest in
many countries in the potential of such programmes despite a number
of serious problems Temporary Migration Programmes (TMPs) have
entailed in the past. To improve their performance, Crisp identifies a
number of prerequisites that need to be in place, such as: a clear delin-
eation of the length of contracts, accurate information to (potential) migrants on the terms of TMPs, equal treatment on the labour market,
job protection for nationals, regulation of recruitment agents, rigid inspections and employer sanctions, portable pensions and savings
schemes to enable returns, etc. In conclusion, Crisp notes that an expansion of TMPs is likely to entail a greater regulation of national labour markets, an approach that states may be reluctant to pursue in a
time of general liberalisation of labour and product markets.

Stretching the concept of temporary labour migration to its logical limit, Teun van Os van den Abeelen's 'A new European employment migration policy' proposes a system of temporary employment migration with enhanced options for return migrants to become economically active in their countries of origin. This system involves the admission of temporary workers from selected developing countries for up to five years, complemented by free education and occupational training and a sizeable financial return incentive.[3] This 'investment premium' would be capital accumulated over the working period in the host country through social security savings, pension savings and a share of development aid money and could amount to as much as € 25,000 (including compound interest) for a migrant returning after five years. In addition, there would be schemes for facilitating the productive investment of the return premium, e.g. through business start-up training, tax breaks and complementary micro-credit schemes.

Further elaborating on his previous proposal on managing regular and irregular migration with the 'People Flow' approach, Theo Veenkamp presents new ideas on a composite innovative concept termed 'multiple track partial privatisation of the gatekeepers function'. His presentation 'People Flow revisited: constructive management of changing patterns of migration' relies heavily on private agents ('linking pins' like employers, universities, tourist agents, etc.) in the decision-making on admission, while confining the role of governments to supervision and screening on security and health risks. Potential migrants are offered the choice between three tracks. The first track is for target-oriented migrants who have an evident counterpart in the recipient country (like employers) and who can be processed directly by the linking pins. The second track addresses potentially irregular migrants who can simply register with a newly established temporary work agency and are provided with a totally new residential status as 'explorers'. This status offers only a modest net salary excluding social security or pension benefits. The difference between the net salary and the 'normal' gross salary that employers have to pay is administered by the agency and is used for covering basic health care, education and other costs. The third track is meant for potential refugees, termed 'protection seekers'. Improvement of the effectiveness of this track becomes possible when many explorers who are now clogging asylum systems are tempted away to their own – and for them, more profitable – track.

Noting that arguments over migration often represent a form of social conflict, Franck Düvell suggests in his presentation 'Towards sustainable migration policies' the application of Sustainable Conflict Resolution (SCR) strategies in disputes over migration. This method suggests the inclusion of as broad a number of stakeholders as possible –

and particularly the migrants – into the process of migration policy-making. After discussing the use of fundamental principles of SCR in migration disputes, Düvell suggests a step-by-step approach tackling wider conflicts along separate issues, with the conclusion of partial agreements before moving on to more comprehensive issues. He also notes that reaching consensus on a contested issue does not imply the attainment of all possible goals one may wish to reach. Rather, a nego-tiated settlement implies the finding of a compromise formula through 're-framing' techniques that leaves everyone around the table better off than they would be without a negotiated solution. The challenge lies in identifying possible settings for the application of SCR strategies where 'non-zero-sum solutions' could be found and implemented.

Also applying a bottom-up approach to migration issues, albeit from a different perspective, Jonathan Chaloff asks if the notion of 'Co-devel-opment' – when applied to migration – is 'a myth or a workable policy approach?' He starts from the premise that new forms of mobility and circular migration (transnationalism) can be positive factors for co-de-velopment and observes, somewhat counter-intuitively but by now widely accepted among migration researchers, that a secure residence status that leaves open the option to return ('back and forth rights') can foster circular migration, rather than narrowing the migratory project into early settlement. When it comes to policy options, rather than placing the burden for co-development on single migrants, investment in the community and migrant networks is seen as the better option, as not all migrants are ideal candidates to become development agents. Here, capacity-building and training may help to identify those few agents who really can make a difference. In addition, institutions in the home country must be strengthened in order to make better use of the skills of returning migrants. Finally, co-development links are seen to be especially promising between specific groups and limited areas ('translocal' links).

A rather provocative proposal that challenges the lack of evidence-based policymaking in the migration field is made by John Davies in his 'Imagining policy as a means to innovation: The case for mobile middle-aged'. Based on the study of Albanian elderly who have been re-duced to mere recipients of remittances by their offspring abroad, hav-ing become inactive long before retirement age and faced with the con-sequences of a 'care drain', Davies calls for free movement rights for those over the age of 50. Having their elders join young migrant fa-milies abroad would have a number of advantages: better management of family income and childcare resulting in higher female labour force participation, stronger links with countries of origin passing on culture and language skills to grandchildren and leading to more returns, more social stability and lower crime, etc. On the other hand, it was ac-

knowledged that such a policy would also have to deal with several negative effects: higher health costs for the elderly, more social inequalities, less integration, etc.

While protection issues have been acknowledged by most presenters
as important and valid concerns to be taken into account, Judith Kumin's presentation on 'In-country "refugee" processing arrangements:
a humanitarian alternative?' is the only proposal included here that
tries to tackle protection issues directly. In her view, states have a moral, if not a legal, obligation to offset progressively restrictive control
measures with alternative means of providing protection to persons in
need of it. At the same time, traditional resettlement arrangements
from countries of first asylum are increasingly viewed as problematic
due to their 'pull' effects and their negative impacts on voluntary repatriation. In this context, Kumin argues that 'orderly departure' arrangements directly from countries of origin (as currently already practiced
in certain states by the United States and Canada) may provide a humanitarian alternative for European states and an alternative to irregular migration for migrants in distress.

In the view of Jeroen Doomernik, measures to control migration at
the (external) borders have failed to prevent unwanted migration while
having a number of negative consequences, such as forcing migrants
to invest high amounts on overcoming barriers to migration, thereby
increasing profits of migration facilitators and discouraging return and
circular migration. Instead, in 'Open borders, close monitoring', he
presents the case for open borders, coupled with an internal control
system of close monitoring through registration in a comprehensive
biometric database. In this proposal, the regulation of migration is left
to the labour market, while demands on the welfare state are strictly
tied to contributions (taxes, social security payments, pension accounts,
etc.). Once registered, there would be no more grounds for exclusion
from the territory, unless there are good reasons for it (such as security
reasons or a criminal record). Hence, issues like irregular migration,
human smuggling and fraudulent asylum applications would become
a thing of the past.

The issue of irregular migration and human smuggling is also at the
heart of the proposal put forward by Michael Jandl in his presentation
'The Development Visa Scheme revisited'. The basic idea of this
scheme is the selling of legal entry permits (Development Visas, or
DVs) at prices at or around the prevailing smuggling fees to anybody
who cannot get another type of 'free' visa (e.g. for study or tourist purposes) and who is not explicitly excluded from the scheme (e.g. for past
violations of migration rules). Visa quotas, prices, length and terms
would be based on realistic demand and are to be set annually for each
eligible source country by the EU Council of Immigration Ministers,

who also decides upon the distribution of visas among host countries. The visa fee is divided into three equal parts and is used for development projects, social security/health care expenditures and a return incentive payable upon return of the migrant to the home country. The scheme is complemented by an elaborate plan for monitoring, safeguarding and evaluating performance and outcomes.

Last but not least, a proposal for 'Pricing entrance fees for migrants' was put forward by Holger Kolb along the lines of an argument made by economist Gary Becker. In this proposal, a fixed price is charged for the right to immigrate, which is set according to the calculated costs of the consumption of public goods (welfare benefits, health care, congestion, etc.) by the immigrant and is subject to only the most basic prerequisites (health and security check, no criminal record). Adjustments to the price would be made for accompanying family members and for temporary migration. The system would be efficient as market mechanisms would take care of the selection of migrants, the entrance fee would lead to a positive self-selection of productive migrants and banks would be willing to extend credit for financing entrance fees for high-potential migrants. Providing legal entry channels would also lead to less irregular migration, reduce control costs and cut down extensive immigration bureaucracies.

A little quote before we start

The first ICMPD/IMISCOE workshop on Innovative Concepts for Alternative Migration Policies, held in Vienna on 24 and 25 March 2006, was designed as a first explorative attempt at developing much needed innovative ideas for migration policymaking. In this sense, the preceding call for papers and the workshop itself were a big success already, which was followed up by a widely distributed policy brief and is now complemented by the full written contributions of the authors in the following chapters. To be realistic, it is not very likely that the policy innovations proposed in this book will be implemented soon. But we may find hope and encouragement in this little quote:

> Make no little plans. They have no magic to stir men's blood and probably themselves will not be realised. Make big plans. Aim high in hope and work. Remembering that a noble, logical diagram once recorded will not die. (Daniel H. Burnham)

Notes

1   Michael Jandl is Senior Research Officer at the International Centre for Migration Policy Development (ICMPD). The views expressed in this article are those of the author and participants in the workshop only, not those of ICMPD, as a Vienna-based intergovernmental organisation, or of its member states.

2   An eleventh presentation with a focus on remittances was given during the conference and is recounted in the conference report. However, as this presentation was not followed up by the submission of a paper, it is not reflected in this chapter. My discussion of the ten policy proposals roughly follows the chronological order of their presentation at the workshop.

3   As indicated in the conference report, following several comments from workshop participants, the originally proposed length of temporary employment of seven years was changed to five years in the final version of the paper.

Temporary Migration Programmes: potential, problems and prerequisites

Jeff Crisp, UNHCR[1]

Introduction

A Temporary Migration Programme (TMP) can be described in simple terms as one that enables the citizens of one country to take up employment in another on the basis of a fixed-term residence and work permit.

Such programmes come in many different shapes and sizes. Some offer short-term or seasonal contracts, whereas others enable people to work in a foreign country for several years. Some involve relatively small numbers of highly skilled personnel, whereas others provide employment for large numbers of manual or domestic workers. Some TMPs are negotiated between states on a bilateral basis, whereas others are managed by private sector employers and recruitment agents. Irrespective of these differences, TMPs have an important common denominator: they do not provide migrants with any entitlement to permanent residence in their country of employment.

TMPs attained particular prominence between the 1940s and 1960s, when labour shortages prompted the United States to admit large number of Mexicans (through the Bracero programme) and Germany to recruit workers from Turkey and other countries on the fringe of Western Europe (the *Gastarbeiter* or guestworker programme).

From the early 1970s onwards, however, the industrialised states exhibited declining interest in the establishment of TMPs, partly because their need for foreign labour had been reduced by the downturn in the global economy, and partly because of growing evidence that many 'temporary' migrants wanted to stay on a long-term basis in their country of employment and, if possible, to be joined by family members from their country of origin.

Since that time, TMPs have been most prevalent in the oil-rich countries of the Gulf, where large numbers of short-term contract workers are recruited from Asia, poorer countries in the Middle East, and to a lesser extent, from Africa.

In the past few years, there has been a renewed degree of interest in TMPs, both from industrialised states such as Australia, Canada, Italy,

Spain, the United Kingdom and the US, and from migrant-sending countries such as Bangladesh, Pakistan, the Philippines and Sri Lanka.[2]

In its recent report to the UN Secretary-General, the Global Commission on International Migration (GCIM) also endorsed the notion of TMPs, recommending that 'states and the private sector should consider the option of introducing carefully designed temporary migration programmes'.[3] Significantly, this recommendation was broadly endorsed by The Economist, which described it as 'the most consequential' in the GCIM's report. 'The logic of temporary migration,' it concluded, 'appears irresistible'.[4] The following sections of this article look more closely at that logic.

Absorbing surplus labour

One of the most important outcomes of TMPs would be to provide a means of providing jobs and better incomes to the growing number of people in developing countries who are unemployed or underemployed. As the GCIM report points out, the world's economy is currently expanding at some 4 per cent a year, generating trillions of dollars in new income and lifting millions of people out of poverty, especially in the new 'giants of globalisation', China and India.

But this record of economic achievement has not yet been reflected in the creation of new employment and livelihoods opportunities in other developing countries, where high fertility levels are leading large numbers of young people to enter the labour market. According to the ILO, in 2004, some 185 million people around the world were unemployed. Over the previous ten-year period, the industrialised states were the only ones to experience falling unemployment rates. In every other region they either remained stable or increased.

Such statistics are symptomatic of the fact that the globalisation process has been highly uneven in its impact. According to UNDP, the gap between living standards in richer and poorer parts of the globe is growing. In 1975, the per capita GDP in high-income countries was 41 times greater than that in low-income countries and eight times greater than that in middle-income countries. Today, high-income countries have per capita GDPs that are 66 times those of low-income countries and fourteen times those of middle-income countries.

Because they are unable to find adequately compensated livelihoods at home, increasing numbers of women and men in developing countries are looking for employment opportunities elsewhere. And the incentive to migrate appears to be getting stronger. In many developing countries, market-oriented reforms have made it more difficult for people to find work, especially if they lack education and training.

This trend seems likely to continue. Some 1.3 billion people – around half of the work force in developing countries – are currently employed in agriculture, usually as small farmers. These farmers are confronted with multiple disadvantages. They face competition from subsidised farmers in more prosperous parts of the world. Efforts to market their goods and improve productivity are often hampered by the poor physical and financial infrastructures that exist in many developing countries. A growing number of small farmers must also cope with the problem of environmental degradation, as well as the appropriation of agricultural land by the state and private enterprise.

Growing numbers of these people can be expected to migrate (or attempt to migrate), initially from rural to urban areas and subsequently to other countries. In some states, as the following section explains, this trend seems certain to be reinforced by government policies that are designed to promote the migration of their citizens.

Economic and political returns for countries of origin

For countries of origin, TMPs present a variety of economic and political attractions, the most important of which is the opportunity to increase the flow of remittances that migrants send back to household and community members that they have left behind. In recent years there has been a remarkable expansion in the volume of remittances sent home by international migrants. While accurate figures are hard to obtain, the World Bank estimates that the annual value of formally transferred remittances in 2004 was about $ 150 billion, representing a 50 per cent increase in just five years.

Remittances are now close to triple the value of the Official Development Assistance (ODA) provided to low-income countries and comprise the second-largest source of external funding for developing countries after Foreign Direct Investment (FDI). Significantly, remittances tend to be more predictable and stable than FDI or ODA. They continued to rise during the Asian financial crisis, for example, even as flows of FDI fell.

This is not an isolated case. Evidence collected by the World Bank indicates that when a country encounters political or economic difficulties, citizens who are living and working abroad support their compatriots by increasing the amount of money they send home. In many recipient countries, remittances now play an essential role in sustaining national and local economies. Remittances that are transferred formally can provide an important source of foreign exchange to recipient countries, boost the capacity of the financial sector, help to attract subsequent investment and provide some leverage for sovereign loans.

Remittances evidently provide the most direct and immediate benefits to the people who receive them, many who, the World Bank has established, are amongst the poorest members of society. Remittances
help to lift recipients out of poverty, increase and diversify household
incomes, provide an insurance against risk, enable family members to
benefit from educational and training opportunities and provide a
source of capital for the establishment of small businesses. When remittances are used to purchase goods and services, or when they are
invested in community-based projects or in ventures that demand labour, they also benefit a broader range of people than those who receive them directly from relatives working abroad.

The benefits of TMPs for migrant-sending countries do not stop
there. First, there is an expectation that people who work abroad for a
period of time will eventually go home, taking new skills, qualifications
and connections with them, thereby enabling countries of origin to
compete more effectively in the global economy.

Second, migration, even on a temporary basis, facilitates the growth
of overseas diaspora communities that are ready and willing to invest
in their homeland, whether through the establishment of new enterprises and trading companies or the transfer of knowledge and technology.

Third, the economic benefits of migration have an important political spin-off. If unemployment levels can be reduced and incomes increased, and if a country's more dynamic and enterprising citizens can
be given the opportunity to live and work abroad, there is a reduced
risk that the population will be attracted to political and religious movements that have a revolutionary or radical agenda. Indeed, the Minister
of Labour in the Philippines, one of the world's largest providers of
temporary migrants and contract labourers, acknowledged in a meeting
of the GCIM that, without large-scale migration, the potential for political and social turmoil in her country would be considerable.

Finally, it must not be forgotten that migration also brings significant benefits to those people who are able to find work abroad. Migrants who move from lower to higher income economies are often
able to gain an income that is 20 or 30 times higher than they would
be able to gain at home.

While living costs are usually much higher in countries of destination, most migrants can still earn enough to support themselves and
send remittances home to members of their household and community. By migrating, moreover, people who are living in precarious economic and political circumstances are able to insure themselves and
their families against market volatility, political crises, armed conflicts
and other risks. In countries of origin, temporary migration enables

households and communities to minimise their risks and maximise their opportunities.

When it takes place on the basis of organised programmes, temporary migration also enables people to move to, and remain in, a destination country without encountering the costs, dangers and inconveniences associated with irregular migration and the submission of unfounded claims to refugee status.

Significantly, UNHCR, the UN's refugee agency, has suggested that states should establish new programmes for safe, legal and temporary migration, thereby averting the bureaucratic delays and public hostility that ensues when significant numbers of migrants use the asylum channel as a means of gaining access to the labour markets of the industrialised states.

Meeting labour needs in the industrialised states

The renewed interest in the establishment of TMPs is based to a significant extent on the assumption that the industrialised states will in the future become increasingly dependent on foreign personnel. This assumption is rooted in demographic realities.

Many of the world's more prosperous states now have fertility levels that are below the replacement rate of 2.12 per woman. Their populations are becoming both smaller and older, a situation which threatens their ability to sustain current levels of economic growth and to maintain their existing pensions and social security systems. In contrast, virtually all of the world's population growth is taking place in developing countries. According to the United Nations Population Division, fertility rates for the period 2000 to 2005 range from just 1.4 in Europe and 2.5 in Latin America and the Caribbean, to 3.8 in the Arab states and 5.4 in sub-Saharan Africa.

Statistics compiled by the World Bank indicate that the global labour force will rise from 3.0 to 3.4 billion in the period 2001 to 2010, an average increase of 40 million per year. Some 38 million of that annual growth will come from developing countries, and only two million from high-income countries. On the basis of current trends, by the end of the decade, some 86 per cent of the global labour force will come from developing countries.

Thus, if the industrialised states need workers to compensate for the diminishing size of their populations, to provide care to their growing number of elderly people and to support their pensions and social security systems, it will not be difficult for them to fill those gaps through the recruitment of migrant labour from other parts of the world.

The demand for such labour appears to be increasingly strong. In many of the industrialised states, the increasing competitiveness of the global economy has placed new pressures on both private and public sector employers to minimise costs and to maximise the use of cheap and flexible labour – precisely the kind of labour that migrants are able to provide. The growth of migration from poorer to richer countries will not be confined to low-income workers.

The industrialised states are also confronted with shortages of personnel in high-value and knowledge-based sectors of the economy such as health, education and information technology. Unable to recruit, train and retain the necessary personnel at home, a growing number of governments and employers are turning to the global labour market in order to meet their human resource needs.

As the proponents of TMPs point out, for many of the industrialised states, temporary migration presents a more effective and acceptable means of meeting their labour market needs than the long-term or permanent settlement of foreign nationals. Migrant workers, they point out, eventually age and become economically inactive themselves, and so the industrialised states would have little to gain by offering them indefinite residence rights. With the possible exception of traditional immigration countries such as Australia, Canada and the US, the recruitment of long-term workers from other parts of the world would also prove socially and politically unacceptable.

As demonstrated by recent events in countries such as Denmark, the Netherlands and the UK, there is a growing sense amongst the electorate that earlier immigration and integration policies have failed, with the result that the members of many migrant and ethnic minority communities are economically and socially marginalised, and that they have failed to adapt to the values, customs and cultures of the societies in which they live. In the current climate of hostility to the permanent settlement of migrants, temporary migration programmes have an added attraction as a means of balancing supply and demand in the global labour market.

Overcoming the constraints and limitations of TMPs

It would be misleading to suggest that there is any kind of unanimity concerning the potential of TMPs. Indeed, commentators from a variety of different political perspectives have highlighted the constraints and limitations associated with such programmes.[5]

First, and as indicated already, it has become received wisdom to suggest that 'there is nothing more permanent than a temporary migrant'. According to this argument, based to a considerable extent on

Germany's experience with the guestworker programme, migrants who are recruited on a temporary basis have a natural tendency to become accustomed to the life and standard of living available to them in their country of employment.

The only means of averting such a scenario is to employ the draconian forms of control exercised by countries in the Middle East, which make it impossible for temporary workers to take up longer-term residence in the country where they are working, and which entail a total ban on the admission and residence of spouses and other family members.

Second, human rights activists have argued that temporary migration programmes inevitably lead to the creation of a second-class category of worker whose wages, conditions, rights and entitlements are inferior to those of nationals. Working on a similar assumption, other commentators have suggested that temporary migration programmes exert a downward pressure on wages, obstruct the introduction of labour-saving technology and avert the need to maximise the labour force participation of women, members of ethnic minorities and citizens who prefer to live on welfare benefits rather than seeking employment.

Third, in situations where states regulate the employment conditions of temporary migrants, so as to ensure they are not underpaid, overworked or exposed to hazards in the workplace, there is a distinct risk that employers (especially small-scale enterprises and sub-contractors) will turn to the irregular migrant workers and the informal labour market in order to meet their need for workers.

Finally, while acknowledging the important role that remittances play in many migrant-sending countries, a revisionist argument suggests that the poverty reduction and developmental impact of such transfers have been exaggerated, and that the social costs of large-scale migration have been given insufficient attention. According to this argument, most of the migrants who are able to find work abroad are also obliged to leave behind a spouse, their children and other family members whose lives may be seriously affected by the absence of the principle breadwinner.

If these constraints and limitations are to be addressed, TMPs must, in the words of the Global Commission on International Migration, be 'carefully designed'. In practice, that would require the following ten prerequisites to be met.[6]

1. Temporary migrants must be fully informed about their rights and conditions of employment prior to their departure from their country of origin, especially the requirement that they must return to that country once their contract has expired.

2. Temporary migrants must be treated in the same way as nationals with respect to their wages, working hours, health care and other entitlements.
3. Temporary migrants must be given the right to transfer from one job to another during the period of their work permit, thereby enabling them to respond to changing labour market conditions and to avoid a dependence on unscrupulous or exploitative employers.
4. Countries of origin must monitor the implementation of the work permits and contracts provided to temporary migrants, with a view to blacklisting states and employers that violate the provisions of such documents.
5. Countries of destination must prosecute employers who fail to respect the conditions of service offered to temporary migrants or who employ irregular migrants without valid work permits. Such countries must also be prepared to undertake the removal of irregular migrants and temporary migrants who continue to work after their contract and residence permit has expired.
6. Countries of origin and destination must licence and regulate the activities of private agents who are involved in the recruitment of temporary migrants, so as to ensure that they are not subjected to fraud, exploitation or abuse.
7. Countries of destination should grant visas to temporary migrants that will enable them to travel easily between the country where they are working and their country of origin, thereby assisting them to keep in regular contact with their family and community.
8. Countries of origin and destination should cooperate in the introduction of measures that facilitate the reintegration of temporary migrants when their period of employment has expired and they have returned to their country of origin.
9. Countries of origin and destination should consider, and cooperate in, the introduction of portable pensions and social security entitlements, which enable temporary migrant workers who have paid into such schemes to benefit from them once they have returned to their country of origin.

Conclusion

This article has sought to demonstrate the economic, demographic and political logic that underpins the international community's new interest in the introduction of temporary migration programmes. That logic is in many senses a strong one, and yet historical experience suggests that TMPs often give rise to a variety of different negative and unintended consequences, affecting countries of origin, countries of destination and temporary migrants themselves. Indeed, one eminent migration scholar has gone so far as to suggest that all guestworker programmes fail to some extent.

Perhaps the most serious question to be asked about the potential for TMPs concerns the policies of the industrialised states. The globalisation process has hitherto been characterised by an important contradiction, in the sense that it has promoted the cross-border flow of goods, services, capital, information and ideas, but has not generally allowed for a similar movement of people from one continent to another, even when there is a demand for their labour. To the extent that the global labour market has been liberalised, it has been restricted to specific categories of highly valued personnel (finance experts, IT specialists, health care personnel, academics and sports stars) or, at the other end of the labour market, has taken place on a *de facto* basis, by means of irregular migration and informal employment.

The introduction of carefully designed TMPs would represent an important step in the direction of a *de jure* liberalisation of the global labour market. And yet, as argued in the preceding section, a number of prerequisites must be met if such programmes are to be both effective and equitable in nature. A striking characteristic of those prerequisites is that they generally entail a greater degree of state intervention in national labour markets, and increased governmental scrutiny of private sector employers and recruitment agencies. Such an approach may well prove unpalatable to stakeholders that have in recent years placed such a high value on the deregulation and privatisation of the economy.

Notes

1   Jeff Crisp is Special Advisor on Policy Development and Evaluation at UNHCR and former Director of Policy and Research at the Global Commission on International Migration.

2   Since this paper was presented at the ICMPD workshop in March 2006, three new studies on TMPs have been published: Manolo Abella's 'Policies and best practices for management of temporary migration' and Philip Martin's 'Managing labour migration: temporary worker programmes for the 21st century', both papers prepared for the International Symposium on Migration and Development, Turin, Italy, June 2006; and Stephen Castles' 'Back to the future? Can Europe meet its labour needs through temporary migration?' International Migration Institute (Oxford), Working Paper No. 1, 2006.

3   *Migration in an Interconnected World: New Directions for Action* (2005), Report of the Global Commission on International Migration, Geneva, 16.

4   'Be my guest', *The Economist*, 6 October 2005.

5   Some of these constraints and limitations are discussed in Don DeVoretz's 'Temporary migration: an overview', a paper presented at the Third International Metropolis Conference, Zichron Yaacov, Israel, 1998.

6   For an elaboration of these prerequisites, see Martin Ruhs' 'The potential of temporary migration programmes in future international migration policy', paper prepared for the Policy Analysis and Research Programme of the Global Commission on International Migration, September 2005, (www.gcim.org).

A new European employment migration policy

Teun J.P. van Os van den Abeelen, ACVZ

The issue

1. Economic immigration in prosperous parts of the world is as old as civilisation itself, and this is especially the case in respect to the prosperous parts of Europe.
2. Economic migration is a result of the large differences in prosperity and perspective in different parts of the world. It is more than likely that if the differences in prosperity were not as large as is currently the case, migration would be so limited that it would only need policy-based attention from the point of view of the public order and national security. An indication to support this statement is the limited inter-country migration (approximately 2 per cent) within the EU between fifteen countries that have a reasonably comparable prosperity level and the increase in economic migration now that, as a result of the expansion of the EU to 25 countries, a number of economies have joined in which the average family income is considerably lower than the EU average or the average of the most prosperous EU countries.
3. The urge to escape poverty and a hopeless future is so large that if prosperous countries have very restrictive economic immigration policies, people will try to enter these countries and obtain employment by unlawful means (the asylum channel, fake family formation, illegality).
4. Unlawful methods of circumventing restrictive immigration policies result in serious problems.
   The unlawful use of the asylum channel is so considerable that the vast majority of asylum seekers registering in (Western) Europe cannot make a successful appeal to the Refugee Treaty. The temporary reception of these asylum seekers and the assessment (and rejection) of their asylum requests, including the subsequent procedures and deportation, cost the EU many billions of euros; this is wasted money.
   Fake family formation is the practice of a 'paper' marriage or the realisation of a forced marriage. Both these practices aim to make it possible for a person to enter the EU country with the objective to

stay in that country with the 'partner' for so long that it becomes possible for the person to obtain right of residence. Both these forms of unlawful family formation are detrimental. Entering into a 'paper' marriage without actual cohabitation is quite simply fraud, and it makes it impossible to conduct any check on the working capacity of the person involved – which of course is the issue in employment migration. Furthermore, this practice creates black money, because persons willing to facilitate a paper marriage demand large payments.

Forced marriages often generate immense suffering and, by their nature, may result in domestic violence.

Illegality results in undeclared employment and therefore frequently in the exploitation of the illegal immigrant who is mostly unable to enforce her or his rights. It also results in social misery, because illegal immigrants are unable to live and participate in everyday society. In the case of illegal families, these problems are carried forward to subsequent generations.

It is not possible to prevent all the abuse and unlawful use of immigration regulations. Reality forces us to acknowledge that eliminating the illegal arrival and stay of immigrants has proven impossible. All the experiences with the phenomenon of illegal immigration in the past few decades throughout the world lead us to the conclusion that it is physically impossible to create a 'Fortress Europe'. It would need a George Orwell to maintain a society in which only controlled residence is possible.

However, this awareness must not lead us to the conclusion that it is pointless to have any border controls at all, nor to resign ourselves to the existence of illegal immigration. For the reasons we indicated above, illegal immigration is and always will be a phenomenon that must be prevented *as much as possible*. This is – particularly in Southern European countries – really only possible if an alternative is offered.

The need for employment migration

5. Without immigration, the EU as a whole will be showing a strong decline in population numbers after 2020. The average number of births in the EU is 1.4 per woman, while 2.2 births are needed to maintain the population at its current level.

   In densely populated areas a considerable reduction in the (working-age) population may be beneficial in the long-term, but in the short-to-medium term it may, in many cases, cause serious economic problems (a drop in demand, production stagnation and a lack of financing options). There will generally also be social problems in the form of a shortage of care facilities for the relatively higher number of senior citizens. With respect to the years 2010 to 2040, these problems are increased further by the additional ageing of the population in that period; the proportion of elderly in the total population will increase more because there was strong population growth in the years 1945 to 1960. Not all countries in Europe experienced these phenomena to the same extent. The birth statistics per country differ somewhat. Furthermore, a reduction in the proportion of working-age people in relation to the total population becomes more serious for a country if its old-age facilities are financed by means of a 'pay-as-you-go' system rather than by fully funded schemes. The seriousness of the problem is also linked to the remaining options a country has for increasing labour participation. For instance, the Netherlands has a relatively low proportion of female labour participation. Increasing the labour participation of women can somewhat increase the options for supporting a relatively large number of economically non-active people in society.

Finally, when posing the question of whether immigration, in any form, has a positive effect on the aforementioned problems, the population density is relevant, insofar as it can lead to (part of) a country becoming so overpopulated that it can result in infrastructural problems. Within Europe this could be the case for (parts of) the Netherlands, which has the second-highest population density, and perhaps also for the German Ruhr area.

6. Despite intercultural and social problems relating to non-Western European residents, in Europe there is, generally speaking, no major resistance against the immigration phenomenon.

7. This point can be substantiated by the fact that nearly all countries in the EU have a very restrictive economic immigration policy in respect to non-EU citizens whilst, at the same time, the EU as a whole and the individual countries within the EU open their borders wide to highly educated and knowledgeable migrants. The attitude appears to be: immigration is not a problem as long as we also benefit from it.

The proposed temporary migration system for employment

8. The above considerations lead to the conclusion that, in the first place, it is necessary to reduce the prosperity discrepancies in the world, not only from the point of view of general fairness, but also to effect a structural improvement of the immigration situation.

A substantial part of the solution to this problem lies outside the scope of migration policy and will have to be achieved by means of trade measures and through strengthening the economic, social and political position of a number of (developing) countries. A lot of material has been written on this subject, and this is not the place for in-depth proposals in that direction. Furthermore, most development economists agree that breaking down customs restrictions and removing trade barriers are the main measures needed, as well as ones the rich Western world is refusing to consider because of a narrow sense of self-interest or as a result of national political considerations.

However, in addition to these measures it is possible to make a contribution to resolving the problems of both immigration countries and developing countries by means of specific measures laid down in the immigration policy. To this effect, a system of temporary employment migration must be realised, with enhanced options for returning employment migrants to become economically active in their country of origin.

9. From a global point of view, a system of temporary employment migration accompanied by enhancement of the economic and social position of those returning to their country of origin can have a significant positive effect if the system is applied on a large scale. It is therefore desirable that the system is introduced by the EU as a whole. In addition, it must be possible to fine-tune the system per country not only for the support base, but also because of the competences of the different countries and the differences in local situations. Because it is not possible to find a legal basis for such a system within the EU as it currently exists, the whole must be documented in a separate supplement to the EU Treaty.

10. This system of temporary employment migration from developing countries accompanied by a considerable enhancement of the position of those returning to their countries in order to give these countries an economic boost can – very briefly – be described as follows:

   – Temporary workers are admitted for a period of time not exceeding five years, based on the anticipated shortages in labour supply for each country in the EU and without the option of resettlement elsewhere in Europe within this five-year period. The individual countries will each determine their immigration quotas.
   – A selection of these temporary workers, particularly from those developing countries, will benefit from a knowledge/financial boost. The selection is based on the assumption that workers are literate, and may also incorporate a requirement to meet

minimum requirements in respect of professional knowledge and/or experience.

- Payment of an investment premium is made upon actual return to the country of origin (after a maximum of five years). This investment premium can be financed by using three sources, namely:
  (1) a reserved old-age pension contribution;
  (2) funds that are released because of adjustments to the social security package; and
  (3) a contribution from development aid funds.
- Free education for temporary workers, either on-the-job training or training in addition to their work, contributes to better economic opportunities in their country of origin.
- It must be possible to attach the possibility of obtaining mini-/meso-credit to this investment premium if, in the country of origin, the premium is invested in such a way that it will also generate work for one or more persons who are not relatives.
- Introduction of a European Benefit Entitlement (Residents Status) Act (which excludes illegal immigrants from any assistance apart from elementary medical aid and education for illegal minors), supplemented by the stipulation that anyone found to be working illegally will be declared an undesirable in Europe. This means that a subsequent illegal stay for employment purposes becomes a punishable offence for this group, and it will become impossible for them to legally enter Europe for an extended period of time.
  Furthermore, it may be possible to come to agreements, at a European level, with developing countries that want to participate in these temporary migration arrangements about the accelerated return of any nationals of these countries who are staying in Europe illegally.
  At the same time, a European system of criminal and economic sanctions must be put in place for private individuals and companies that provide employment to illegal immigrants.

Clarification of the temporary migration system

The temporary nature of the employment migration prevents a strong increase in the population, which actually prolongs the problems associated with the ageing of the population and makes the shortage of workers a problem that continues to recur on an increasingly large scale. Once the 'grey wave' has abated after 2040, the immigration quota can be reduced. With a little optimism and especially also by assuming that an effective system of measures – also in the area of commercial policy – will be realised within a reasonable period of time, we may trust that some 35 years from now, the developing countries will have acquired a better economic position, which means that the prosperity discrepancies will be smaller. This means that, by then, the 'need' for illegal immigration will no longer be felt as strongly as it is at present.

The entire system described above is based on the assumption that the temporary workers will actually return to their country of origin after their contract period has expired. Experiences with temporary employment migrants in Europe so far show two different pictures:

(1) In the public opinion, the image of the guest workers from the Sixties and Seventies in a number of (Northern) European countries, whose stay was supposed to be temporary but who never left, is strongest. Because no efforts were made with regard to the language skills and integration of these guest workers, social problems continue to exist until today, even for the subsequent generations.

(2) A lesser known fact is the reality that, at present, the large majority of recent employment migrants in the Netherlands return to their country of origin, even if they are ultimately allowed to stay permanently.

In addition, the temporary nature can be overcome by family formation with someone who is allowed to stay permanently in a European country. Partly because of the stipulations in Article 8 of the European Convention on Human Rights (ECHR) it is not easy to legally eliminate this phenomenon among this group. All of these factors highlight the need to guarantee the temporary nature of the stay in some other way.

The investment premium, which is one of the cornerstones of this temporary migration system, will – in view of the scope of the savings in pension expenditure and social security premiums (including compound interest) to be achieved over a five-year period – result in quite considerable amounts of money. (The chosen period of five years is in accordance with the EU regulations about long-staying third-country nationals). If a substantial part of the amount that most European countries spend on development aid is used differently, this amount can once again grow considerably. All in all, based on a rough and not yet fully substantiated estimate, we are probably looking at a premium of € 25,000 – or more. This amount is so high that every non-knowledge worker will want to comply with the temporary nature of the system in order to be allowed to receive the premium with investment credit, which will only be paid out in the country of origin and possibly in a number of yearly instalments.

All in all, this is a good starting position to build a reasonable existence in the country of origin, especially if compared to all the losses if
temporary migrants do not comply with the obligation to return to
their country of origin. This would support the assumption that the
system will not be burdened by illegal 'overstay' on any significant
scale.

The fact that countries in the EU continue to have a say about the
immigration of non-EU workers is inherent in this proposed system of
temporary immigration. The quota that they determine for this scheme
only has direct consequences for their own employment market and
the economy.

The proposed system has a range of advantages for the countries of
origin. Assuming that we are talking about many thousands of workers
for each country of origin, the investment premium and the additional
credit option will, together, create a serious impulse for an improvement of the economy of the country in question. An additional advantage is the fact that, this way, part of the development aid funds will
end up with the enterprising part of the nation, and only if, and to the
extent that, they actively use these funds for investment in the economy.

It is likely that in the case of temporary employment migration on a
serious scale, not only highly or vocationally educated persons are
required and/or usable. To increase the economic value of the migrant
upon her or his return, both to the country of origin as a whole and to
the person in question, the proposal provides for the possibility to give
all temporary employment migrants additional training. This training
must be based on the existing work and mental level and on the work
to be performed in the temporary employment country. Consider, for
instance, on-the-job training for employees as well as education provided by existing educational institutes.

The system does not take into account the fact that before a more
evenly distributed prosperity will start to reduce immigration, there will
always be an urge to come to Europe illegally, because most citizens of
developing countries are not in a position to get a job as a temporary
employment migrant.

However, because in this system part of the illegal immigration in
some EU countries will no longer be deemed inevitable and therefore
tolerated and periodically 'regularised', it will be possible to agree and
enforce considerably stricter measures to combat illegal employment
migration for the whole of Europe. In this case a regularisation ban
would be a realistic option. Making a repeated illegal stay or an illegal
stay after return an offence, on the basis of this temporary arrangement across the EU, will contribute to reducing illegal employment migration.

And finally

The plan outlined above creates a combination of a flexible system of employment migration with a form of effective development aid. It is clear that the details of such a system need to be further defined and that there will no doubt be problems associated with this solution. For instance, it is obvious that a 100 per cent return rate will not be realised, and that it will be particularly difficult to guarantee the actual investment in premiums and credit without resorting to an enormous bureaucratic monitoring system. Neither can it easily be guaranteed that the developing countries will not use unlawful means to try to divert part of the investment premiums to the government coffers or the pockets of corrupt officials.

Problems are there to be resolved in order to realise desired solutions. Without new ideas and daring plans the world will remain where it is today. Hopefully, this plan can contribute to preserving Europe's prosperity whilst making a contribution to the realisation of a fairer distribution of prosperity in the world.

People Flow revisited: constructive management of changing patterns of migration

Theo Veenkamp, DEMOS

Introduction to the updated People Flow approach

The 'People Flow Report'[1] (May 2003) was a first attempt to design the outline of an approach to international migration that would be less defensive and more constructive than usual. It was set up as a thought experiment, culminating in first sketches of a number of innovative concepts for alternative migration policies. There was much demand for the report, and it generated lively discussions in a number of conferences on 'openDemocracy'[2] and in other ways. Since then, the approach as first described in the report was further adapted and refined in view of the many comments and suggestions made and my own ongoing thinking on the topic.

In September 2005 the Global Commission on International Migration (GCIM) launched its report 'Migration in an interconnected world: New directions for action'.[3] In important ways, the search direction of the Global Commission is the same as that used by the authors of the 'People Flow Report'. In other, equally important ways the People Flow approach seems to be more innovative, especially on implementation strategies. I will use therefore the report of the Global Commission as the main reference point when sketching the updated People Flow approach.

Changing patterns of migration

The People Flow approach was developed on the basis of an analysis of major migration trends, on the one hand, and typical government policy reactions to these trends on the other hand. For a short and up-to-date overview of these trends the report of the Global Commission on International Migration forms the best possible source. In this report the following major trends are mentioned:
a. 'Human mobility is not only becoming larger in scale and scope, but also more complex in nature' (page 7).
b. 'The old paradigm of permanent migration settlement is progressively giving way to temporary and circular migration' (page 31).

c. 'The Commission calls on states to acknowledge the fact that many migrants with irregular status have found a place in their economies and societies (page 38).
d. 'The notion of the socially or ethnically homogeneous nation state with a single culture has become increasingly outdated. Most societies are now characterized by a (often high) degree of diversity' (page 42).
e. 'A study prepared by the UN Population Division concluded that the integration of migrants in host societies depends primarily on their command of the national language, their ability to find reasonably paid work, their legal status, participation in civil and political life, as well as their access to social services' (page 45).
f. 'As a result of the globalization process and the growth of transnational communities, established notions such as citizenship and the nation state are being redefined. In the future, it seems likely that a growing number of people will have more than one nationality, will identify with more than one culture and will divide their time between more than one country' (page 47).
g. 'The distinction between voluntary and forced migrants has become increasingly blurred' (page 75).

Unchanged control-oriented reflexes of governments

The key conclusion of the 'People Flow Report', departing from basically the same trends as the Global Commission, is that the dominant reflex of governments in reaction to ever-changing patterns of migration is to develop ever-changing mechanisms of control. But control is a dangerous illusion. It is either not really effective, or, when it seems effective, creates bigger and bigger problems because of unforeseen and unwelcome side effects. A new approach is necessary.

The analysis of the Global Commission of the responses of governments to the changing patterns of migration is less penetrating and more diplomatic, but this does not stop the Commission from drawing the following rather sharp conclusion:

> ...the international community has failed to capitalize on the opportunities and to meet the challenges associated with international migration. New approaches are required to correct this situation.

From defensive migration control to constructive people flow management

When one is convinced that it is necessary to look for new directions, a well-considered choice for main departure points is crucial. The Global Commission makes clear choices in this respect:

a. Capitalise on the resourcefulness of people who seek to improve their lives by moving from one country to another.
b. Ensure that the increased scale of migration brings real benefits to countries of origin, countries of destination and to migrants themselves.
c. Move from sovereignty-as-control to sovereignty-as-responsibility.
d. With the scale and scope of international migration growing, countries and communities must seize the opportunity to make the most of their diversity.
e. Coherent policies begin at home.

The authors of the 'People Flow Report' in some respects use other language and emphasis, but basically, there is major agreement on the search direction for new approaches. The Global Commission makes one additional choice: protection of human rights. This aspect is hardly dealt with in the 'People Flow Report' because a really constructive approach to migration leads in and of itself to substantially fewer problems when dealing with the consequences of human rights violations.

New policy directions and the implementation issue

It is inspiring and encouraging that the Global Commission and Demos share almost completely the relevant trends, the conclusion that new approaches are necessary and the main departure points for looking for new policy directions.

The Global Commission ends with recommending the following six major policy objectives.

– Create better conditions in a globalising labour market for migrating out of choice rather than necessity.
– Reinforce the economic and developmental impact of migration.
– Address irregular migration.
– Strengthen social cohesion through integration.
– Protect the rights of migrants.
– Enhance the governance of international migration through more coherence, capacity and cooperation.

The 'People Flow Report' uses, in part, different terminology but basically shares these objectives. But in a very crucial way, the People Flow approach starts where the Global Commission ends. The authors of the 'People Flow Report' think that not only new policy directions are necessary, but also that, at least for some of the objectives, innovative implementation strategies are necessary. Otherwise, these objectives simply cannot be realised. For this reason, enhancing migration governance through more coherence, capacity and cooperation – the last of the six objectives – is certainly necessary, but unfortunately not sufficient. The core ambition of the People Flow approach is therefore not only to turn to new policy directions, but in addition, to look for innovative implementation strategies in those cases where clearly required.

The People Flow approach

In order to increase the chance to hit upon implementation strategies that are both innovative and workable, seven innovation search principles were chosen in the 'People Flow Report'. These (partially reformulated) search principles are:

1. Go back to the essential meaning of what migration is.
2. Understand and accept the reality of migrants' motives and the mixed feelings of arriving and receiving population.
3. Connect with the most recent thinking and practical experience concerning effective public management of complex processes in dynamic environments.
4. Frame new paradigms that correspond to the changing reality and open up the mind, preferably those that are already emerging and 'in the air'.
5. Try to discern underlying patterns in the growing complexity of migration and look for the most suitable 'levers' for exerting real influence.
6. Liberate governments from the trap of rising expectations and diminishing results by looking for better mixes of what governments really should do and others can do just as well or even better.
7. Make the best possible use of modern technology.

The People Flow approach could be best described as constructive flow management driven. Governments should rely less on (border) control and more on flow management. 'Flow management' does not mean moving with the flow, but, instead, using, channelling and redirecting strong migratory 'undercurrents' intelligently by understanding the behaviour patterns of different types of migrants and their 'counterparts', as well as by connecting with their underlying motives in constructive and inventive ways.

The core innovation: multiple track partial privatisation of the gatekeeper's function

In the original 'People Flow Report' a number of innovative concepts were launched for 'multiple flow management'. Now, three years and many comments and suggestions later, one core innovative concept emerges as a serious suggestion for implementing in an unorthodox but workable manner two major objectives recommended by the Global Commission:
– Create better conditions in a globalising labour market for migrating out of choice rather than necessity.
– Address irregular migration.

Moreover, this innovative concept is designed in such a way that at the same time a third Global Commission objective is being served:
– Reinforce the economic and developmental impact of migration.

The core innovative concept can be labelled as: 'Multiple track partial privatisation of the gatekeeper's function'. This concept is based on two design principles:
1. Rely for deciding on admission to cross the border more – but not totally – on private linking pins in international networks.
2. Provide potential migrants with three migration tracks from which they can choose: one for target-oriented migrants, one for explorers and one for protection seekers.

Partial privatisation of the gatekeeper's function

The first design principle is a translation of the innovation search principle to look for better mixes of what governments really should do and others can do just as well or even better. The essence of the international border concept is the gatekeeper's function: who is allowed in and under what conditions. Traditionally, this is one of the vital roles of cooperating national governments. It should remain so for the key reasons governments have been doing this from the beginning: protecting the security and health of those who are in. But there has always been a third reason: protecting national economic interests. The enormous increase in international mobility and the ongoing globalisation of national economies require us to change our thinking in this respect. For two reasons: first, national economic interests are more and more served by dynamic cooperation in international networks. Second, the overwhelming majority of admission decisions are of a routine nature.

Therefore, a new approach should be developed on the basis of the following choices:
- Rely for deciding on admission, except for the security and health aspects, on private linking pins in international networks like employers, university administrators, tourism operators, etc.
- Cooperating governments should develop more mobile and technologically advanced methods for screening on security and health risks.
- As for the rest, the role of governments should be focused on:
    (1) supervising the admission activities of the linking pins;
    (2) maintaining an emergency back-up function for dealing with flows that cannot be handled by the linking pins;
    (3) providing certain information and other facilities in the public interest.

Separate tracks for target-oriented migrants, explorers and protection seekers

The second design principle, choice between three migration tracks, is meant as an answer to the blurring distinction between voluntary and forced migration and – related to it – the elusive problems of irregular migrants and refugees.

The first track – meant for target-oriented migrants – is basically a familiar one. It is to be used for all those potential (voluntary) migrants who know what they want and have an evident counterpart in the recipient country. These migrants and their counterparts can greatly profit from the proposed partial privatisation of the gatekeeper's function, because in a much more flexible and efficient manner a great variety of ever-changing flow patterns can be accommodated.

The second track is the unorthodox one. It is primarily meant for the potentially irregular migrants. The first choice that I have made here is to look for a new paradigm that defines this category in its own terms instead of ours: explorers. For that is how they see themselves: leaving home behind in order to explore better perspectives for life and for whom the question of whether they do this out of choice or necessity is a rather academic one. They do not know exactly what they want, and they have no evident counterpart, except for a friend or an uncle to whom it is difficult to say 'no'. These explorers are in many cases pioneers who try to settle into an upward perspective rather than a country. The second choice is to create a totally new residential status for this category that only offers them what they really need and that protects those with a classical residential status against unfair competition from the explorers. This explorer status comprises among others the following elements:

- registration at a private temporary work agency set up especially for explorers;
- a modest net salary;
- a gross salary that is, in principle, the same as for regular employees doing the same work;
- no taxes, no social security, no pension scheme;
- the difference between net and gross is administered by the agency and can be mostly used for basic health care, basic education, buffer for short temporary unemployment, travel costs, etc.;
- help with sending of remittances.

The private agencies work under the supervision of the government migration service in a way that is comparable to the private linking pins. The agencies can have real or digital branch offices in countries where many potential explorers live. The underlying idea of this special track for explorers is to give potential irregular migrants realistic information about their chances and, if they want to come, convince them to register at one of these explorer agencies, simply because the package of costs and benefits is more attractive than when being an irregular migrant. An important condition for the success of such a track is that there is a strict regime for irregular migrants, making it very unattractive to choose the irregular migration option.

The third track is the one for refugees. Also here, I prefer to use language that describes more precisely the underlying motives of the potential migrants. What the international community has committed itself to in the Geneva Conventions is to offer those that really need it more than as a refuge or hideaway: protection by a responsible and decent government. If we look carefully, for the category of protection seekers, too, new varieties and new patterns of movement are emerging. Until now, this development has been partially blocked from view because large numbers of explorers clog the tracks that are meant for protection seekers. One of the key underlying ideas of the composite innovative concept of the multiple track partial privatisation of the gatekeeper's function is of course to improve the effectivity of the first two tracks to such an extent that the third track is really open to those who first and foremost are in need of protection. If that were the case, it would become possible to explore in a more relaxed manner ways to improve the effectivity of the protection track in view of the emerging new variety of protection seekers and their movements. Also here, I think there are interesting possibilities for new divisions of tasks and roles between governments and, in this case, especially NGOs.

The necessity of multiple people friction management

The concept of multiple track partial privatisation of the gatekeeper's function is an innovative elaboration of the need for 'multiple people flow management'. People flow inevitably leads to all sorts of people friction that must be addressed in a variety of ways: multiple people friction management. That is not only important for the sake of social cohesion. Citizens will give their governments more leeway for constructive migration policies that rely less heavily on control if these governments have proven to be effective in constructive people friction management. This link between flow and friction management is an important element in the People Flow approach. Multiple people friction management seems at first glance a rather self-evident concept. But in the political arena, this concept may look much more problematic when one realises that it requires different friction management approaches for target-oriented migrants, explorers and protection seekers. 'Integration' becomes less and less suitable as the umbrella concept for friction management policies aiming at maintaining social cohesion because ongoing migratory movements are increasingly diverse in numbers, nature and patterns. Rather, a toolbox of policy instruments seems necessary, including a variety of formal residence statuses, to be applied in a tailor-made manner as the specific situation and context requires. Fortunately, especially in larger metropolitan areas in Europe, interesting experiments in tailor-made friction management are taking place. And if we have to be innovative in this respect too, it pays to look for them with the help of the seven innovation search principles that were identified earlier on.

Concluding remarks

The innovative policy implementation strategies presented above are described only sketchily. Basically, I have formulated a composite cluster of partially new concepts, with terse explanation and illustration. That is how I want it to be, because it is primarily intended as a specimen of a new way of thinking. It is up to researchers, practitioners and policymakers to test, scrutinise and improve this way of thinking until specific and workable proposals emerge. I want to conclude with a few general underlying arguments that could be helpful in such an endeavour.

First of all, a key element is the possibility for potential migrants themselves to choose one of the three tracks. This is crucial in view of the trend that the distinction between voluntary and forced migration is becoming increasingly blurred. Therefore, instead of governments going out of their way trying to decide which migrant fits which category, let the potential migrants decide for themselves.

Second, the innovative conceptual cluster is not developed on the assumption that its adoption would guarantee the complete disappearance of irregular migration or no explorers choosing the protection-seeker track. That would mean a new dangerous illusion of perfection and control. The underlying assumption is, nevertheless, that it will make a real difference in two ways. First, because it is a constructive approach, promoting social cohesion instead of polarisation, creating energy instead of destroying it, using talents instead of wasting them, reinforcing the economic and developmental impact of migration instead of diminishing it. Second, because policies will substantially be more workable and sustainable – not more simple. As in so many other public domains, if things become more complex, solutions have to become more sophisticated. The policy goals can be – and increasingly have to be – simple in the sense that they must appeal directly to basic human needs and aspirations. At the same time, we must allow for very sophisticated implementation strategies that reflect the underlying complexity and changing dynamics in a workable way.

In view of all this, I am well aware that testing, scrutinising and further elaboration of the conceptual cluster as presented above will take a number of years and will generate a lot of complications and dilemmas of its own. The key question is, however, which complications we prefer in the end.

Notes

1   Theo Veenkamp, Tom Bentley & Alessandra Buonfino (2003), 'People Flow, Managing Migration in a New European Commonwealth', Demos/openDemocracy, London.
2   www.opendemocracy.net.
3   'Migration in an interconnected world: New directions for action' (2005), Global Commission on International Migration, Geneva, available at www.gcim.org/en.

Towards sustainable migration policies

Franck Düvell, COMPAS

Applying principles of mutual cooperation and sustainable conflict resolution strategies in disputes over migration: a methodology for addressing the migration dilemma

Introduction

This paper aims to move beyond conventional and exclusive migration policies that are considered ethically questionable.[1] It also criticises more recent moves towards migration management as no more than another version of regulated closeness repeating many of the usual unjust practices, but even more so, for the structural exclusion of migrants from decision-making processes. And finally, present interpretations of the principle of 'freedom of movement' are rejected, too, for their radical individualism that miss ideas of political regulation and control. Instead, because migration is analysed as a social conflict, a method is suggested and applied that aims to address the conflict by way of sustainable conflict resolution, which is characterised by integrating all stakeholders and that includes migrants into the decision-making process, and which is based upon consensus processes for the mutual benefit of all. SCR does not suggest solving the conflict once and for all; instead it is a method by means of which conflicts could be addressed one by one, as they arise. Finally, it will be shown that embryonic SCR processes already exist in several countries.

Migration conflicts, failing controls and dissatisfying concepts

In September 2005, on several occasions hundreds of migrants engaged in fighting with Moroccan and Spanish border guards in an attempt to enter the Spanish exclaves of Ceuta and Melilla, both in legal terms EU territory.[2] Several migrants were killed and hundreds injured. In previous years, similar events, ranging from cat-and-mouse games to open fights, though on a lower scale and raising less publicity, were reported from the US-Mexican border, from Australian waters, from Greek-Albanian border regions and from German-Polish borders. Immigration restrictions, as they are, provoke divergence and are often undermined as high numbers of irregular immigrants in Western societies illustrate. The present systems of migration control are frequently considered inefficient,[3] expensive,[4] not making sense[5] and being ethically problematic. These incidents and other examples illustrate that the relation between migrants and enforcement authorities – or in other words, between mobile and sedentary populations – often takes the form of open conflicts.

In order to address conflict and inadequacy, two contrasting policies are suggested – managed migration and freedom of movement – respectively liberalising migration. Both shall be briefly assessed in their likely impact. Several 'managed migration' models have been suggested such as the New International Regime for Orderly Movements of People (NIROMP),[6] the General Agreement on the Movement of People (GAMP)[7] or People Flow.[8] These are supposed to be less exclusive, less restrictive and less confrontational regimes. The ideas are then responded to by bodies such as the International Organization for Migration (IOM), the Berne Initiative, the Geneva Migration Group and some national governments.

A specific feature characterising all these models, policy processes and suggestions is that migrants are by and large excluded from the policymaking processes; if at all, they may be granted an observer status, but only that. Finally, a close look reveals that the 'regulated openness', which Ghosh[9] claims for his proposal, rather is a form of regulated closeness.[10] Managed migration rather seems to be a euphemism for still strict regimes which would inevitably result in ongoing irregular migration and continuous conflicts and does therefore offer neither a satisfying nor a sustainable solution.

Alternatively, freedom of movement shall be considered. Whilst in pre-state time free movement was natural, determined by ecological conditions and limited by natural barriers only, in pre-nation state times, and during the first globalisation about five hundred years ago,[11] migration occasionally became a normative right.[12] This changed again with the emergence of Westphalian-type states during the 17th century and more so with the emergence of the modern nation-state during the late 19th and early 20th centuries, when migration became a challenge and successive restrictions were introduced. Particularly in late-modern times, rights of emigration and rights of immigration have been perceived as increasingly irreconcilable, both were thought to be 'morally asymmetrical'[13] and considered an antagonist 'right versus right' constellation.[14] Meanwhile, corresponding to a new era in globalisation, the trend in migration discourse seems to have swung back again like a pendulum, since an increasing number of scholars argue for some right to migration. Based on moral equality, arbitrariness of place of birth and the suffering exclusion, Bauder[15] questions the legitimacy of immigration controls; Carens[16] and Hayter[17] argue for 'open borders'; and Cohen[18] claims that 'no one is illegal'. In particular, under conditions of increasing global integration, authors such as Pecoud and Guchteneire[19] suggest a 'migration without borders' scenario, whilst activists all over the world call for a world with 'no borders'.[20] Economists, too, analyse migration restrictions and come to very similar conclusions, though from a different perspective. They argue, for example, that liberalised migration would generate an enormous thrust in growth, which would benefit all,[21] or that free migration would equalise an otherwise unequal distribution of global wealth and must therefore be seen as a major precondition for global distributive justice.[22]

Three major criticisms can be made: 1) few of these works indicate what an adequate political framework could look like. Most of the arguments presented are of purely normative, though plausible, nature; 2) freedom of movement cannot be looked at in isolation from other issues, because migrants often move out of misery and often end up in misery, and from that perspective it offers no solution; and 3) embedded in the present interpretations of 'freedom of movement' is a form of radical individualism, as a consequence of which migrants and sedentary populations in the receiving countries are put into a situation of unfettered and unregulated competition, which could even be envisaged as some sort of chaos, and there would be, as there are now, winners and losers.

From these arguments, it can be concluded that: 1) a conflict requires adequate, and in the best case, sustainable politics to be resolved, hence sustainable conflict resolution strategies; 2) the exclusion of mobile populations from policymaking processes will not lead to appropriate solutions – instead, the conflict will remain. Therefore, thinking must concentrate on how to best integrate the migrants into the process of migration policymaking; 3) freedom of movement is acknowledged for its plausible normative arguments but should not be understood as 'free' in terms of the absence of regulations. Instead, it requires political mechanisms and a framework within which people can exercise this right; and 4) in order to ensure that freedom of movement will be for the benefit of all, and to satisfy principles of distributional justice, it requires a system of compensation.

The model sketched here introduces principles and means of sustainable conflict resolution into the conflict over migration. It is aimed to overcome the dissatisfying elements of migration management, addresses the equally dissatisfying aspects of the freedom of movement concept and, as an alternative, suggests an integrated framework aiming to reconcile the two concepts.

Sustainability and sustainable conflict resolution

It is surprising that the principle of sustainability and, in particular, sustainable conflict resolution, which has become so prominent over the past two decades, has not yet been applied to migration matters even though it has been made fruitful in many other areas:

> The acceptance of 'sustainability' as a practical policy goal and the increasing use of consensus-based processes in the resolution of a broad array of ...disputes are two important trends. ... [Sustainability] is about dealing with people and their diverse cultures, interests, visions, priorities, and needs.[23]

Participation of all stakeholders is a precondition to sustainability according to the Brundtland report.[24] Within this context, a stakeholder 'is a group or organisation who has influence in a particular area of policy or who is affected by policies'.[25] Meanwhile, stakeholder participation has become an imperative; according to UN sources 'everybody or anybody who is affected by or benefits from any development endeavour must take active part in its planning, decision-making, and implementation'.[26]

Another precondition for sustainability is consensus, reached through a process of communication, and defined as no less than unanimous agreement. This, however, does not imply that all stakeholders find all their aspirations satisfied. Instead, a considerable level of compromise may be required from all parties: 'consensus processes share one common feature: interaction among participants is face-to-face with the goal of arriving at mutually acceptable outcomes or decisions'.[27] A consensus-based process seems to be of particular value in cases where contrasting interests and values have already reached conflict or even crisis level. Because both crisis level and exclusion of migrants have been identified as crucial features of the present migration dilemma, sustainable conflict resolution again seems to offer an alternative.

Amongst the requirements mentioned for successful consensus processes are:

> 'Reciprocal recognition and respect for the values of other parties', 'tolerance ...and respect for the people who hold them. The goal is to try to develop outcomes that enable the parties to live together in spite of their differences, not to eliminate these differences'; The necessity to 'find a way that meets the needs of all parties'; 'Solutions and agreements must be technically, fis-

cally, socially, and culturally [and one needs to add economically] viable'.[28]

Meanwhile, ten principles of sustainable conflict resolution strategies have been identified,[29] namely: 1) purpose-driven; 2) inclusive; 3) based on voluntary participation; 4) self-designed; 5) flexible; 6) offering equal opportunities and 7) respect for diverse interests; 8) accountable; 9) committed to time limits and 10) to effectively implement and monitor the agreement.

SCR reflects various crucial values and principles, such as moral equality, diversity, respect for the other and their interests, inclusiveness, democracy and self-determination.

The most commonly applied method of SCR is a round table joined by all significant stakeholders. This is enriched by inputs of experts, possibly led by a mediator, and accompanied by side meetings, hearings, special sessions, public meetings, information meetings and transparent public relations work. The round table setting is designed to tackle otherwise unequal power relations, which shall thereby be neutralised.

Several of the conditions characterising SCR epitomise basic liberal principles. For example, Rawls develops his 'Theory of Justice'[30] from a sort of round table meeting. Ackerman suggests a 'dialogic principle', which is based upon the 'neutrality principle', meaning that in the course of a dialogue moral ideals of the opponent should not be questioned. Finally, game theory-based constitutional political economy[31] also emphasises stakeholder participation, consensual processes and suggests that a conflict is best dealt with by mutual cooperation.

Inherent to SRC is the reframing of methodology, because at a round table facts are presented by all stakeholders, as well as looked at from different perspectives. This may result in typically held assumptions and concepts being radically changed:[32]

> Seeing a conflict from the other parties' perspectives – learning about their pressures, concerns, and difficulties – helps open minds to creative problem solving. Equally important, the effort may encourage a reciprocal effort from the other parties.[33]

What offers the most promising outlook when imagining the application of those principles to the migration conflict are ideas of 'working together' ('as equals'), 'designing a [political] process', 'maximizing the ability to resolve differences' and to 'reach a consensus' with which 'all participants are willing to live'.[34] In the following section, these principles shall be applied to issues over migration.

Applying sustainable conflict resolution principles to migration

Several areas can be identified in which SCR dialogue seems to be an adequate method to address conflicts over migration issues, for example:
1. when people feel the need to migrate, but before they actually make a choice where to go and before they actually leave;
2. when migrants turn up at the border of another political community;
3. when migrants are already inside a community other than their community of origin;
4. when migrants wish or ought to return or move on to another destination.

According to Principle 1, governments, for example, may first need to acknowledge that combating unwanted migration seems to represent a no-win situation,[35] whereby migration control budgets increasingly reach unbearable levels[36] and are ethically questionable.[37] A precondition is that all parties are dissatisfied with conventional processes and simultaneously realise that the time is right for alternative procedures. Unfortunately, often 'stakeholders lack the ability to identify the issues of their conflict',[38] and one of the very first efforts should be put into identifying the entire scope of the conflict, possibly with the assistance of professional conflict resolution practitioners. Migrants may take as a starting point that, even though they make it to their destinations by the million, the result is often not what they came for. Employers may need to take on board social, political and cultural arguments. And trade unions may want to acknowledge that migrants are often workers in the first instance and are therefore perfectly potential members.

With respect to Principle 2, the guiding question is: 'who should be presented?' It may be practical to distinguish between inner and outer circles of stakeholders. The former group consists of those who are most, and directly, affected and the latter group encompasses those who are least, and only indirectly, affected.[39] If, at a later stage, new stakeholders are identified or emerge, they shall be included at that point.[40] This means that any party participating in, and affected by, migration processes should participate, such as sending and receiving countries (their respective governments), mobile and sedentary populations, non-migrating family and community members left behind, employers, mobile and immobile employees, social partners, civil society and international organisations. Even reluctant parties may join, since otherwise they would lose their chance to influence the outcome. And also protests are a necessary strategy taken by some stakeholders to 'gain a seat at the table'.[41] No stakeholder shall be excluded because of legal arguments ('we do not talk to *sans papières* because they are illegal immigrants and are not supposed to be here') or on financial grounds ('we cannot participate because we lack the resources to come to the meeting'). What is appealing here is the consequence, in that migrants and indigenous populations have a chance to meet face to face.

Still, there remains the problem of unequal power, as states or corporate agencies usually have more resources and, for example, as governments have more formal authority. However, once a SCR process has been entered, this is usually on the basis that conventional means of conflict resolution have failed and that a SCR process appears more promising. Consequently, a SCR process can only become successful, if migrants' representatives are treated in a fair and principled manner (Principle 6). Paradoxically, a weak party gains more power by being recognised and by being given legitimacy by a more powerful party. As yet, migrants' power basically rests upon human agency, the power that forces state stakeholders to enter into negotiations, but once migrants are acknowledged as partners in a SCR process, they additionally gain political power. The main power which migrants gain is to veto in case they feel treated with disrespect or unfairness, or in case they disagree with the solution on the table.

Instead of uniformed processes, the organisational culture of each stakeholder must be acknowledged; time and space must be allocated to each stakeholder to consult with their constituency as often and, long as necessary; and equal access to experts' opinions must be granted (Principles 5, 6 and 8). The process must be fair, open and equitable, as its prospects would be jeopardised by unequal power relations in which, for example, the interests of migrants would be suppressed by the interests of other stakeholders, such as the representative of a nation-state. Finally, a learning opportunity is in-built here.

Furthermore, because migrants are the party frequently stereotyped as 'floods', 'scroungers' or 'threats', they must be given the opportunity (Principle 6) to give a true picture of their reasons and values (for example in televised workshops), and thereby have the opportunity to indirectly address the opponents' constituency. But the destination countries' communities, of which migrants may have stereotypes ('roads are paved with gold'), have equally good reasons to explain that not all of them are rich and comfortable, but that not few of their members are poor, uneducated and unemployed or otherwise less able, and therefore fear competition from migrants. Combating stereotypes and misunderstandings is essential to any SCR process and in particular to its subsequent implementation.

The actual challenge lies in the diverse interests (Principle 7). Governments may argue 'we have a right, the sovereignty and the mandate of our constituency to control and limit those aiming to enter our national territory'. In contrast, migrants may argue 'we should have a right to come and go as we please'. Multinational businesses may argue 'we wish to recruit the best, the brightest or the most diligent from wherever they are in the world', whilst small businesses and employers may argue 'we wish to be protected from additional competition',... and so on. These arguments are expressions of different values, different interests and different perspectives leading to an adversarial relationship. Mutual respect for each party's values, such as the demand for freedom of movement or some control over those wishing to become members of a territorially bounded community, is a precondition in order to prevent a dispute from becoming a destructive and unsolvable struggle. All parties must be prepared to step back and acknowledge the other parties' values, interests and perspectives, and to understand the reasons behind them.

When it comes to the end of SCR processes (Principle 9), common ground shall be identified and an agreement reached. It may, nevertheless, be practical to withhold from holistic solutions and instead give way to partial agreements, where consensus might be reached; simultaneously, it may be wise to leave disputed issues, where for the time being no consensus could be reached, for a later round. Instead of aiming at the design of a comprehensive though rather sophisticated global migration policy, a step-by-step approach tackling the conflict along separate issues can be envisioned. All parties, however, will only accept this if it is agreed that within a reasonable time frame all aspects are dealt with.

Suggestions for implementation and examples of SCR processes in migration

At the end of an SCR process an implementation route and its monitoring procedures shall be defined. Successful implementation of an agreement is more realistic in proportion to how much all stakeholders have been involved, accept the agreement and support its implementation. Top-down processes contradict the very principles of SCR. Only where all parties are involved is there a chance that the agreement will finally be accepted, disseminated and defended, as well as implemented.

It may be adequate to consider the creation of new institutions, which cannot be associated with any of the conflicting stakeholders and which therefore have the potential to make a fresh start and to engage the conflict constructively.[42] That means that, for example, reforming an existing institution, such as IOM, ILO or UNHCR, or even only providing it with an extended mandate, may not be adequate. In that sense the Global Commission on International Migration, as initiated by Kofi Annan in 2003, was an encouraging move in principle, though this was only established on a temporary basis.

Consensus-based SCR processes may not necessarily be thought of on international or national levels only; it may well be worthwhile considering regional and local levels, such as negotiations between would-be migrants and the actual local community. They may also be applicable to individual functional systems of society only, such as labour markets or welfare institutions. Finally, they may be applicable to conflicts of only limited nature. SCR processes, and specifically their implementation, may well be combined with suggestions to regionalise migration policy. Instead of envisaging how to get all relevant stakeholders of whole countries around a table, the process could begin from the observation that usually it is not countries but regions that are linked through migration,[43] and because of this, it would be better to invite stakeholders of these regions to SCR processes.

There are examples where migration issues have been dealt with by local SCR-like procedures. In Switzerland, for instance, concerns related to social and human rights issues, as well as regularisation procedures, have been addressed by way of regular consultations, which involved collectives of irregular migrants, cantonal government and other public authority staff in Lausanne, Fribourg and Basel. In Italy, it has been found that migration links towns in Lombardy with towns in Senegal. Meanwhile, communities in both sending and receiving towns get engaged in projects aiming at organising support, channelling resources and supporting return and investment.[44] In Portugal, the government has initiated a round table on migration, bringing together authorities, academics and NGOs. In Brussels, a group of irregular immigrants and their supporters had occupied a church to demand regularisation of their status. Finally, and after a hunger strike had been staged, the Minister for the Interior met with the migrants and NGOs, and after some talks, a process was agreed on for how the dispute could be settled.[45] And in Hong Kong, the Asian Migration Centre (AMC) and the Coalition for Migrants Rights (CMR) hold regular dialogues with the Hong Kong government over issues of regulations.[46] However, further research is required to obtain a clearer picture of experiences and results of such processes.

Conclusion

Sustainable Conflict Resolution is about 'seeing a conflict from the other parties' perspectives – learning about their pressures, concerns, and difficulties – [it] helps open minds to creative problem solving'.[47] Integrated into SRC processes are reframing methods, which inspire innovative solutions. With respect to immigration, the goal is to try to develop outcomes that enable the parties to coexist in spite of their different ways of life, and not to eliminate these differences, or indeed, one way of life. The crucial aim seems to be to find a solution in which no one loses, in which no one is worse off and in which ideally all have gained something. A perfect result of SCR is a 'non-zero-sum' solution in which gains have been made by all stakeholders.[48] Some stakeholders, such as migrants, may have gained freedom, other stakeholders, such as businesses, may have gained economically, and a government may have (re)gained political control over otherwise irregular movements.

Notes

1   Earlier versions of this paper have been presented at the Global International Studies Conference, Istanbul, in August 2005, and an extended version has been submitted to the journal *Ethics and International Affairs*.

2   See for e.g. *The Times*, 30 September 2005.

3   Cornelius, Wayne, Philip Martin & James F. Hollifield (1994), 'Introduction: The ambivalent quest for immigration control', in Wayne Cornelius, Philip Martin & James F. Hollifield (Eds.), *Controlling immigration: a global perspective*, 3-42. Stanford: Stanford University Press.

4   Pecoud, Antoine & Paul de Guchteneire (2005), 'Migration without borders: an investigation into the free movement of people', *Global Migration Perspectives* 27. Geneva: Global Commission on International Migration.

5   Bhagwati, Jagdish (2003), 'Borders beyond control', *Foreign Affairs* 82: 98-104.

6   Ghosh, Bimal (2000), 'Towards a new international regime for orderly movements of people', in Bimal Ghosh (Ed.), *Managing migration. Time for a New International Regime?*, 2-26. Oxford: Oxford University Press.

7   Straubhaar, Thomas (2000), *Why do we need a General Agreement on the Movements of People (GAMP)?* HWWA Discussion Paper 94. Hamburg: Hamburg Institute of International Economics.

8   Veenkamp, Theo, Alessandra Buonfino & Tom Bentley (2003), 'People Flow: Migration and Europe', *openDemocracy* (1 May 2003).

9   Ghosh, Bimal (2000), 'Towards a new international regime for orderly movements of people', in Bimal Ghosh (Ed.), *Managing migration. Time for a New International Regime?*, 2-26. Oxford: Oxford University Press.

10   For an analysis see Franck Düvell's *Illegal Immigration in Europe* (Houndmills: Palgrave/Macmillan), Chapter 11.

11   Hatton, Timothy J. & Jeffrey G. Williamson (2005), *Global Migration and the world economy. Two centuries of policy and performance*, Cambridge, Massachusetts: MIT Press; Dirk Hoerder (2002), *Cultures in Contact*, Durham: Duke University Press.

12   See Josef Bordat's 'Spiel ohne Grenzen. Migration und Welthandel bei Franz von Vittoria (1492-1546)', Paper presented at Conference Grenz//Gänge, 5-7 November 2004, (available at www.gradnet.de/events/papers2004/bordato4long.htm). However, this is not generalisable: for example, local governments developed their own policies towards migrants, and Chinese rulers, from the mid-fifteenth century, restricted any movements (see Hoeder's *Cultures in Contact*).

13   Walzer, Michael (1983), *Spheres of Justice*. New York: Basic Books, 40.

14   Teitelbaum, Michael (1980), 'Right versus right: immigration and refugee policy in the United States', *Foreign Affairs* 1: 21-59.

15   Bauder, Harald (2003), 'Equality, justice and the problem of international borders: the case of Canadian immigration regulations', *ACME* 1: 167-82.

16   Carens, Joseph H. (1987), 'Aliens and citizens – the case for open borders,', *Review of Politics* 49: 251-273.

17   Hayter, Teresa (2000), *Open borders. The case against immigration controls*. London: Pluto.

18   Cohen, Steve (2003), *No one is illegal. Asylum and immigration control, past and present*. Stoke on Trent: Trentham Books.

19   Pecoud, Antoine & Paul de Guchteneire, Op. cit.

20   In several countries, including many EU countries, but also ranging from Ukraine and Belarus, to Canada and Australia, networks of activists of this name exist; see www.noborder.org.

21 Hamilton, Bob & John Whalley (1984), 'Efficiency and Distributional Implications of Global Restrictions on Labour Mobility', *Journal of Development Economics* 14: 61-75.
22 Harris, Nigel (2005), 'Migration and development', Paper presented to 1. Global International Studies Conference, 2-8 August 2005.
23 Cormick, Gerald, Norman Dale, Paul Emond, S. Glenn Sigurdson & Barry D. Stuart (1996), *Building Consensus for a Sustainable Future: Putting Principles into Practice*. Ottawa: National Round Table on the Environment and the Economy, 3.
24 WCED (1987), *Our Common Future: Report of the World Commission on Environment and Development*. Oxford: Oxford University Press.
25 UNED (2001), *Stakeholder Involvement*, Briefing Sheet. London: UNED Forum.
26 UNESCAP (2003), *Stakeholder participation*, United Nations (available at www.unescap.org/drpad/vc/orientation/M6_intro.htm).
27 Fraser, Colin & Jonathan Villet (Eds.) (1994), *Communication. A Key to Human Development*. Rome: Food and Agriculture Organization of the United Nations, 2.
28 Cormick et al., *Building consensus*, 70, 69, 4, 8 (in the order of quotations).
29 Ibid. 7.
30 Rawls, John (1971), *A Theory of Justice*. Oxford: Oxford University Press.
31 Buchanan, James M. & G. Tullock (1965), *The Calculus of Consent*. Ann Arbor: University of Michigan Press; Geoffrey Brennan & James M. Buchanan (1985), *The Reason of Rules: Constitutional Political Economy*. Cambridge: Cambridge University Press.
32 Cormick et al., *Building Consensus*, 53.
33 Ibid. 74.
34 Canadian National Round Table on the Environment and the Economy, quoted in Cormick et al., *Building Consensus*, 4.
35 Bhagwati, *Borders*; Düvell, *Illegal Immigration*.
36 Pecoud and Guchteneire, *Migration without Borders*.
37 Chang, Howard (2003), 'Immigration and the workplace: Immigration restrictions as employment discrimination', *Chicago Kent Law Review* 1: 291-328.
38 Odidison, Joyce (2003), *Sustainable Conflict Resolution – an Objective of ADR processes*. Eugene, Oregon: Mediate.com (available at www.mediate.com/articles/odidisonj2.cfm).
39 Cormick et al., *Building Consensus*, 52.
40 Ibid. 91.
41 Ibid. 12.
42 Shonholtz, Raymond (1993), 'The Role of Minorities in Establishing Mediating Norms and Institutions in the New Democracies', *Mediation Quarterly* 3: 231-241.
43 Düvell, Franck (2006), *Europäische und Internationale Migration*. Münster: Lit.
44 Stocchiero, Andrea (2006), 'Il capitale sociale transnazionale dei migrante senegalese e un vetorre di co-sviluppo?', Rapporto conclusivo della ricerca CeSPI, Rome: CeSPI.
45 Expatica News (2006), 'Asylum seekers end hunger strike in Brussels church', 16 March 2006, (available at www.expatica.com).
46 These examples have been brought to the author's attention by Genevieve Gencianos, in her capacity as Officer of Migrants Rights International, Geneva, in the course of an email conversation from August 2005.
47 Cormick et al., *Building Consensus*, 74.
48 Ibid. 70.

Co-development: a myth or a workable policy approach?

Jonathan Chaloff, CeSPI

'Co-development' has become an important buzzword in discussing and presenting migration policy in Europe. Quite often, however, those using the buzzword have taken advantage of the lack of a specific definition of the concept and have failed to implement policies that truly have a positive impact on development in countries on both sides of migration circuits. A fundamental question therefore is whether co-development principles can find real application in policy. Some recent examples of policy initiatives and innovative practice may provide clear indications for a workable policy approach.

Co-development: the maturation of a catch phrase

Co-development, as a term, emerged from the development cooperation domain and not from the migration domain. It was not until the 1980s that the French began to use the term in association with the growing number of assisted return programmes. However, these programmes were meant essentially to facilitate removals, both by increasing compliance and by providing a sort of ethical excuse for the policy. Looking at these programmes, in fact, it is evident that the primary beneficiary of assisted return was the deporting country and not the receiving country.

In the 1990s, European policy discussions maintained a sharp distinction between development policy and migration policy. The 'root causes' of migration, especially poverty and poor human development opportunities, were underlined as a target for development aid. Repression, conflict and lack of respect for human rights also attracted growing attention as push factors for migration, especially since the 1990s saw increased migratory pressure from conflict zones. This 'root causes' vision of the link between migration and development was enshrined in the EU's 1999 Tampere Conclusions. The 'co-' in Tampere's 'co-development' was never transformed into policy, since later councils and directives had the explicit objective to prevent immigration through security and conditional aid.[1]

The European migration debate, historically dominated by northern European countries whose labour migration policies ended in 1973, began in the late 1990s to take into account the fact of mass labour migration. This was particularly evident in southern European countries, where governments resigned themselves to regulating migration rather than preventing it. A flurry of legislative activity followed, with draft European directives on all aspects of migration.

At the same time, the vaguely worded Tampere conclusions led to a chorus of objections and counter-proposals from civil society, development agencies and researchers. The discussion that ensued allowed for the development of a more detailed and articulated institutional vision of co-development, one which the European Commission attempted to express in a Communication, first in late 2002 (COM/2002/0703 final), and again with a September 2005 Communication still under discussion (COM/2005/390 final). The latter finally concedes that the important element in migration-for-development, given the inevitability of human movement, is how to maximise the positive impact of migration on development in the home country.[2]

The policy environment has therefore matured and begun to assimilate the link between co-development and migration: that the movement of individuals may be supported so as to improve its impact on the home country, and that such development impact may have effects on the receiving country beyond merely reducing migratory pressure.

However, what are the actual examples of migration co-development schemes? What principles underlie the current innovations in this area?

Co-development has been a concern of CeSPI in recent years, and the Rome-based policy research institute has brought together scholars in the migration field with experts in development policy. This ongoing work has both observed and assisted the evolving Italian approach to co-development, and allows for the identification of some concrete indications.[3]

Transnational integration: fostering mobility and circular migration

Many migrants do not intend to emigrate definitively. Migratory projects may foresee a period of work abroad alternating with a return, according to the availability of work abroad and the feasibility of return. This kind of transnationalism, when manifest in circular migration, is a positive phenomenon for co-development because migrants can count on moving back (and forth) when the time is right or when the appropriate resources are available. Education acquired in the host country can be applied in the home country; social and financial capital accumulated during work in the host country can be leveraged into business activity in the home country.

This kind of movement is not acknowledged in current policy. Migration law in most receiving countries rarely takes into account the plans and projects of the migrants themselves. In fact, admission and stay policy is generally developed to meet domestic needs and to address national concerns and issues. For example, short-term visas – from seasonal work to longer but limited admission – are meant to protect the domestic labour market from excess supply in the event of downturns. The policy is meant to facilitate the departure of the migrant, with no consideration of what might happen in the home country upon return.[4]

Sending country governments appear no more sophisticated in their understanding of migrant needs. Negotiation of bilateral agreements places emphasis on increasing access to host country labour markets – essentially opening the pressure valve for domestic unemployment in countries of origin – without considering the characteristics or skills of migrants or their potential return. The immediate interest is in sending the unemployed abroad so that they can send remittances home.

One among few exceptions is the resentment of southern African countries towards the UK for drawing away domestically trained nursing staff.[5] Yet this concern is limited to protecting a dwindling native labour force in a strategic sector, and has not led to a major policy shift towards supporting the return or circularity of these nurses. Nor has this concern about workers in the health sector led sending countries to develop concrete policy measures aimed at reducing the departure of other qualified workers.

Fostering circular migration will require freeing migrants from the obligation to remain indefinitely in the host countries, while ensuring that they can attempt to return to their home countries without losing residence rights in the host country. In other words, any measures which provide security of status favour circular migration. Dual citizenship is perhaps the strongest form of assurance of this right, and the expansion of dual citizenship can be taken as a positive sign in this direction.[6]

One might even cite the EU directive for long-term residents[7] as a means for increasing circular migration. Of course, the trend in European host countries towards granting stability to long-term residents has been sustained by an interest in migrant rights rather than by concern about fostering circular migration. Nonetheless, the effect could be the same. In fact, the long-term residents directive sharply limits the range of action of any future temporary labour schemes: with seasonal work running as much as nine months, and long-term residence granted after five years, temporary work schemes must range between one and five years.

Even procedural changes may affect mobility. Delays in providing visas and permits discourage movement. Students may have to worry about losing their residence rights in the host country if they return home to seek work after graduation.

Some rigid labour laws may unwittingly restrict circular migration. Trade unions in Italy, for example, have struggled with the interest of some migrant members to save their holidays for extended trips to their home countries; likewise, some employers are hostile towards such lengthy absences, even when the holiday has been earned.

Restrictive citizenship, residence and procedural policies force a physical permanence in the host country. The physical permanence not only prevents return, but convinces migrants to narrow the migratory project into settlement. Migrants are forced to abandon plans for return; resources are no longer saved or remitted, but invested in settlement (mortgages and education of children in the host country, for example). A transnational approach, with mobility as an expectation, sees investment in both countries – for example, home purchases in both countries – and the creation of schools which follow the home country curriculum, to exploit advantages of being in-between.

Flexibility in residence – 'back and forth' rights – allows migrants to plan and change their strategies for movement according to changes in conditions in both countries and to changes in the priorities of individuals and families.

A number of temporary migration schemes have been proposed, with the idea of supporting development-friendly circular migration: expiring work visas, development accounts, reimbursable pension payments, etc. One common defect in these proposals is the need to apply one mechanism to all migrants, fixing either the maximum length of stay or the size of the cash reserve for aid or reimbursement. Yet every individual migrant has his or her own target and his or her own limits: a seven-year stay may be appropriate for some migrants, but may be too long or too short for others. Likewise, a € 30,000 return subsidy may be enough for one migrant – to build a rural home, for example – but too little for another – to start a business in a city, for example. Proposals for fixed-length temporary work visas or fixed-sum incentive schemes ignore this fundamental variable, and once again confirm that the host country is more interested in limiting permanent stays than in matching migrant and sending country needs.

Investment in the network and not the individual

Another bromide in the policy discussion is the 'migrant as co-development agent'. That is, that development aid should shift part of its focus from aid-driven development projects to those of emigrants. In this vision, migrants take on the responsibility for development in their countries. This may be through remittances from a diaspora, productive return (assisted or unassisted) or investment. The onus is shifted from the host country to the migrant.

An obvious shortcoming of this approach is that the immigrant himself or herself has not asked to be a development agent, and it isn't fair to expect development to be driven by individuals who have emigrated for themselves and their families, and not for the benefit of their hometown or home country. To expect their remittances to substitute for development aid risks being just a facile excuse for reducing aid commitments. A diaspora may be the starting point for co-development processes, but it cannot be the only actor.

Rather than assigning a role to – and placing a burden on – individuals, emphasis can be placed on improving the conditions of an entire community. Capacity-building is important. IOM's MIDA project,[8] for example, starts by simply providing a network for skilled expatriates, regardless of their migratory projects, and links them with local institutions. The community, as a whole, becomes increasingly aware of development needs and priorities and of the interests of different actors in the home country. These contexts become the source for the emergence of development actors within a community. After all, not all migrants are ideal candidates to become development agents. First, they may not care about their home country. They may not be able to do anything with resources: running projects or launching import-export businesses require medium-to-high qualifications. Even skilled and motivated migrants may choose investments that deform the economy in their home countries, as can be seen in the real estate markets in cities in major sending countries. Resources to the community – especially training and recognition of skills – help identify those few agents who can make a difference, as well as help structure the intervention in a positive way.

At the same time, the community of migrants, as a whole, can be supported in its transformation into a base for co-development. For example, migrant banking initiatives are important: efficient use of economic resources in the host country can lead to reinforcement of formal remittance channels, as well as to increased use of credit mechanisms in the home country.[9]

Of course, it's not enough to create a network. Institutions in the home country must be reinforced, especially for the placement of high-skilled returnees in strategic sectors, such as public administration, universities and hospitals. This may require broader institutional reform. One example of networks and institutional reform going hand in hand can be found in Albania, where an international student association arranges short apprenticeships in public administration and private businesses for Albanian students abroad. There is a reciprocal impact, as students are exposed to job opportunities in their home countries, and institutions measure themselves according to additional standards. Also in Albania, public administration has reduced barriers for returning students and created a set-aside for the foreign-trained, in order to allow returning students to enter public administration.

Refocusing attention from the transnational to the translocal

The Italian example is particularly interesting because of the increasing autonomy of local authorities in development. While local authorities are – as always – excluded from determining admission and stay policies, they are the public bodies that deal with migrants. Migratory chains often link specific areas in sending countries to specific towns in host countries. Co-development links can therefore be made between specific and circumscribed groups moving back and forth between limited areas. Recent CeSPI work on projects linking towns in Lombardy to towns in specific regions of Senegal provide an example of how local communities can be organised, supported and mobilised to channel resources and support productive return and investment.[10] Weak and fragmented migrant associations can be reinforced; even small migrant communities can pool significant resources when seed money, training and validation are provided. Local bodies also appreciate the opportunity to expand economic ties with the source towns of resident migrants.

The possibility of links with local institutions and bodies in the home country increases the chance for success for initiatives. Weak institutions in the home country may be easier to involve when ties are closer, and improved trust in local authorities in the home country leads to greater interest in productive ties.

Some final remarks

Nation-states have developed their migration and development policies without serious consideration of their mutual impact, and it is not realistic to expect host country migration policy to suddenly start worrying about the impact of choices on sending countries. At the same time, sending countries have little experience in fostering return migration and may see migrants as more useful when just sending remittances, rather than returning home and aggravating labour oversupply.

As recent waves of migrants start to acquire permanent residence status, obstacles to mobility are reduced. Yet even when mobility is guaranteed, weak institutions and negative experiences with corruption and misadministration can turn potential development agents away from considering investment or return. Sometimes the conditions in the home country are simply too poor for any co-development. Nonetheless, by reinforcing diaspora communities, a sort of reserve is created, a capital that can be mobilised if and when conditions change in the home country.

Local transnationalism is a promising area of co-development support and policy. Yet the multitude of stakeholders on both sides and the lack of experience with complex international negotiations can make local-to-local development difficult to organise and manage.

There is also a cognitive leap that needs to be made by policymakers. It can be difficult to start to think outside of national boundaries, and most policy is made for people who stay put or who migrate once, and definitively. These are neat categories and provide a clear constituency. Circulating populations defy traditional means for circumscribing constituencies. Yet the transnational context represented by today's migrants – part of the process of business globalisation, institutions, culture and civil society – is another constituency, albeit more fluid. A question remains over who will represent them – and where. The stakeholders who are tapped to represent migrants are usually the most settled.

Finally, free movement of people has just as large an impact on development as free movement of capital. Globalisation of other flows cannot neglect the development impact of the movement of human resources and know-how. The interests of individuals and families for betterment of conditions should not be considered contrary to other development interests, but rather, compatible. This is not to suggest that open borders are the only way to achieve co-development objectives. In fact, the issues discussed in this paper are based on exploiting possibilities under existing migration policy frameworks.

None of the above examples represents 'thinking outside the box' of current migration regulatory paradigms. In fact, the proposals discussed here are examples of 'thinking inside the box', trying to find ways to exploit potential co-development opportunities without having to fundamentally change migration policy. This makes the proposal more politically palatable, but promises no sudden solution.

Notes

1 CeSPI (2003), '*More development for less migration*' or '*Better migration for more development*'? *Shifting priorities in the European debate*, MigraCtion Europa, Periodical analysis bulletin on migration policies in Europe, Special Issue December 2003, www.cespi.it/bollMigraction/MigSpecial3.PDF.

2 Pastore, F. (2006), 'Transnazionalismo e co-sviluppo: "aria fritta" o concetti utili? riflessioni a partire dall'esperienza di ricerca del CeSPI', Discussion Paper produced in the framework of IOM's project Development & Migration Circuits, February 2006, www.cespi.it/SCM/discussion%20paper.pdf.

3 For an overview of Italian co-development policies and projects, with a particular focus on the Mediterranean, see F. Piperno and A. Stocchiero's *Migrants and Local Authorities for the EuroMediterranean Transnational Integration*, CeSPI Working Papers 23/2006, www.cespi.it/WP/WP23-2%20Euromed%20migrants.pdf. See also A. Stocchiero's *Policies and Practices on Migration and Development in Italy: Lessons to be learnt and Suggestions for the EU's Aeneas Programme*, Position Paper CeSPI, February 2005, www.cespi.it/migraction2/Migr&Dev%20positionpaper%20CeSPI.pdf.

4 Regarding the socio-economic reinsertion of former migrants in the country of origin, following forced repatriation, see the results of an empirical research conducted by CeSPI in Albania, Morocco and Nigeria in L. Coslovi and F. Pipern's: *Forced return and then? Analysis of the impact of the expulsion of different categories of Migrants. A comparative study of Albania, Morocco and Nigeria*, Final research report produced for the ALNIMA project (2002/HLWG/26), February 2005, www.cespi.it/PASTORE/Rapporto%20ALNIMA-ENG.pdf.

5 For an in-depth analysis, see OECD, *Trends in International Migration*. 2003 Edition, Organisation de Coopération et de Développement Economiques, Paris, 2004, Part III.

6 Along similar lines is P. Weil's *A flexible framework for a plural Europe*, Discussion Paper prepared for the British Presidency of the European Union, October 2005, www.fco.gov.uk/Files/kfile/Weil-final.pdf.

7 Council Directive 2003/109/EC of 25 November 2003 concerning the status of third-country nationals who are long-term residents. *Official Journal L 016*, 23/01/2004: 44-53.

8 For more information see www.iom.int/mida.

9 Ceschi, S. & J.L. Rhi-Sausi (2004), *Banche italiane e clientela immigrata. Rimesse, risparmio e credito: le iniziative in atto e le prospettive di crescita*. Roma: Bancaria Editrice.

10 See studies produced in the framework of the EU-funded project 'Rafforzamento del capitale sociale nell'ambito del fenomeno migratorio senegalese' (collected at www.cespi.it/coopi-cespi.htm).

Imagining policy as a means to innovation: the case for a mobile middle-aged

John Davies, SCMR

Thinking about migration policy

In this brief paper I argue that migration policy in the United Kingdom is often inequitable and irrational and, as such, provokes non-compliance by the migrants it adversely and irrationally seeks to control. I further argue that such inequitable policy brings the whole system of migration control into disrepute, in that it is not evidence-based but is a contrived application, i.e. a socially constructed device that is intended not to manage migration rationally, but to quell moral panic (Victor 1998) about migrants as dangerous threats to social order and national security. If migration policy is constructed according to such criteria, there is a place for improving such policy by imagining more equitable policy that can be used as effectively for the same purpose. More equitable although irrational policymaking could rebuild a social contract with migrants, in which the migrants could acquire benefits by acquiescing to comply with irrational policy, thus reinforcing the policy as an effective means to control the migrants.

The essential element of establishing such a social contract, which enables an irrational policy to appear to be an effective device for the management of migration, is to offer migrants benefits if they comply or appear to comply with its provisions, or for the policy not to require any change in migrant behaviour or actual practice. Therefore, the most effective imagined policy will be presentable as a means by which to protect the social order and national security while offering migrants benefits to comply with its requirements or the opportunity to avoid the policy with only minor inconvenience so as to not transgress its legal requirements.

In this paper I will catalogue a recent series of UK migration policies that have been deliberately constructed to fit with the need to create a popular imagination regarding the government's effective control of migrants, while actually deliberately being framed to avoid having to engage in any serious attempt to exercise control. While such policies might offer political benefits to the government, they have not really accrued sufficient benefits to the migrants. As such, there could be some value in imagining irrational policy according to the need to quell moral panic that coincidently might offer substantial benefits to migrants, which could then be presented as ensuring social order and improving national security. Evidence can then be used only when required to support such an imagined policy.

Finally, by use of a particular example regarding mobility for the middle-aged, I suggest that by responding to migrants' calls for certain forms of mobility, this social contract might be strengthened by a better-imagined policy for the benefit of migrants and the countries of origin and destination. I conclude that, as much policy is neither evidence-based nor rational, innovative policy proposals from the academic community should not be restrained by considerations of evidence, but can be driven by a creative sociological imagination that uses dialogue to promote equitable policy (Wright 1959; Freire 1970).

Migration is commonly accepted as an issue able to cause alarm and even moral panic when communities perceive that 'others' are likely to intrude on their privileged spaces (Aron 1991). There is often a presumption that such an intrusion will be detrimental to the personal economy and even the security of the citizen (Baldwin-Edwards 2001). Therefore, governments will often expend significant political capital to convince citizens that migrants are being properly controlled and managed (Clayton 2006). The migrants within the UK who are usually considered to require such control are the migrants from the New Accession States (NAS) and the migrants from outside the European Economic Area (EEA) (Cohen, Humphries et al. 2002; Crisp & Boswell 2004). In the UK, the present government has engaged in varied regulation of such migrants through programmes that have been presented as managing or controlling a supposed migrant-related problem (Clayton 2006). However, in many instances the regulations are clearly unable to achieve their declared objectives, and it could be assumed that the regulations were only enacted to represent an appearance of migrant management, and are therefore neither humane nor orderly.

The Worker Registration Scheme (WRS) was intended to 'control' labour migrants from the NAS. The scheme was a £50 tax on such migrants who were required to register with the immigration authority if they were to be employed in the UK. The scheme does not register the large number of self-employed NAS migrants, and as such could not properly count the number of NAS migrants who were coming to work in the UK (Taylor 2006), which was its primary announced function. However, in the UK every new migrant worker is required to register for a National Insurance number and must produce her or his passport when doing so, including self-employed people. As registration is free and will eventually allow the registered applicant to access contributory benefits, many NAS migrants register. This existing scheme could have supplied all the data assembled by the WRS and probably collected superior data as it would have captured many of the NAS self-employed.

More recently, the government tried to prevent many non-EEA migrants from marrying in the UK, so as to prevent such migrants possibly acquiring residency rights in the UK through such marriages (BBC 2005). Restrictions on the possibility of non-EEA citizens marrying in the UK were represented as a serious immigration control policy initiative intended to prevent abuse of UK immigration controls (Browne 2004; BBC 2004). However, the legislation could only restrict marriage through civic ceremonies as the rights of the state church are sacrosanct, and as such any migrant refused permission to marry in a civic ceremony was able to marry in the state church without restriction (Home Office 2005). The government did not monitor such church marriages to ascertain whether they 'increased' in number after the introduction of the controls (Davies 2005). Therefore, the policy could not effectively prevent determined immigration control evaders, and neither did the government try to ascertain if the controls were being evaded by the obvious contrivance of a sham marriage in the state church. Furthermore, the government was specifically warned that the controls were a Human Rights violation (JCWI 2004; BBC 2005). These regulations have now been successfully challenged as such a violation, and consequently, the government must issue permission to marry to all applicants (Casciani 2006). Rather than closing the scheme, the government is requiring migrants to pay £ 135 for a permission to marry, which must be granted (Home Office 2005; Casciani 2006).

Finally, the UK government has decided to place restrictions on Romanian and Bulgarian citizens being employed in the UK once these nations formally join the EEA in 2007 (BBC 2006; Reid 2006). These restrictions were trailed by the government for several months and were presented as consequential to a need to prevent Romanian and Bulgarian organised criminals from coming to the UK and the need not to exacerbate the pressure on some local community resources that have been reported since the influx of hundreds of thousands of earlier NAS – especially Polish – workers (Webster 2006). However, the current Foreign Secretary made it clear that the Foreign Office does not believe that the proposed restrictions will work and that they will only result in an increase in grey market employment during this period. Dølvik and Eldring (2006) published their report on the failure of Finland's robust migrant control regime on NAS citizens by clearly demonstrating the ease by which such controls could be legally subverted by existing mobility rights relating to the posting of workers into Finland by NAS companies. Consequently, Finland has relaxed its control measures.

The Romanians and the Bulgarians have well-established labour migration networks in Greece, Italy and Spain, and it is expected by the Romanian and Bulgarians governments that most migrant labour will head towards those well-established centres (Bobeva 2006). However, once Romanians and Bulgarians have joined the EEA, their citizens will have the right to visa-free travel to the UK, and they will continue to have the existing right to establish themselves as self-employed workers in the UK (BBC 2006). Therefore, it is hard to imagine Romanian or Bulgarian organised criminals intending to operate in the UK being dissuaded by the fact that they will be unable to work for a supermarket or in a London car wash. While inconvenient, this policy offers nothing substantial to prevent any Romanian or Bulgarian from living or working in the UK (Webster 2006); however, it did offer the government the means to claim that it was responding to concerns regarding the new migration from the NAS.

These examples demonstrate that there should be no presumed shared or common agenda between migrants and governments in countries of destination regarding a desire to achieve an equitable migration policy that is humane, rational or even workable. When governments seek to manage migration in ways that are obviously not evidence-based, that abrogate the civil rights of migrants, and are obviously contrivances intended to placate moral panic among citizens at the expense of migrants, there is little encouragement for the migrant to respect or comply with such irrational and inequitable policy. These inequitable and irrational policies represent a moral deficit, in that governments use such interventions seeking to secure only short-term political advantage, rather than implementing evidence-based policy that might produce long-term benefits. Evidence-based policy would allow the migrant involved to clearly understand the rationale of such a policy and even comprehend it as a social contract in which their contribution and value had been carefully considered. Where there is no meeting of minds between the irrational government and the rational migrant, the moral deficit emerges into view as migrants rejecting irrational migration policies and – in the case of NAS migrants – using existing rights to subvert the policy. Irrational policy therefore perpetuates migration contests and crises. It is possible to listen to rational migrants and, by hearing their voices, to construct better contracts between governments and migrants that allow for the meetings of minds that are necessary for any contract to subsist.

An apparently irrational policy proposal

I will now present an apparently irrational policy proposal imagined after discussions with non-EEA migrants whom I have interviewed in regards to other research, and through which some of the problems considered to be current issues in European migration could be addressed. This proposal hopefully demonstrates some of the advantages of listening to migrants when seeking to develop equitable policy that also meets the priority of quelling moral panic. The marriage between the irrational moral panic and a humane policy specifically constructed to quell that panic demonstrates the opportunity to develop a more humane policy incidental to any evidence. Why should irrational policy actually be hurtful or an inconvenience when it could be humane? The most serious indictment of policymakers is not that any policy is irrational but that it is unnecessarily inhumane.

An example of an apparently irrational migration policy that could offer substantial benefits to migrants of a developing country of origin would be the introduction of the death penalty for citizens or others who illegally enter the EEA after transiting the country. Developing countries, such as Senegal, are often accused of not acting aggressively enough to deter irregular migration to the EEA and are often subjected to repeated requests to acquiesce to return agreements. The imposition of the death penalty could be a convenient device by which to demonstrate their commitment to deterring irregular migration from or through Senegal. Forty per cent of Senegalese want to be able to migrate, and they are very likely to use irregular means to enter the EEA. Forced returns from the EEA often involve large opportunity costs for the returned migrants and the loss of any potential for remittances. By introducing the death penalty for irregular migrants who enter the EEA via Senegal, the Senegalese government can claim to be seeking to seriously deter irregular migration while, in fact, actually preventing the return of any Senegalese irregular migrant from the EEA as the return of an irregular migrant to face the death penalty would not be legal in any EEA country because of European Convention on Human Rights (ECHR) obligations. So by introducing a draconian and irrational law that appears to demonstrate a serious attempt to deter irregular migrants, you actually create the means by which such migrants can effectively avoid being returned. If countries of origin are able to use irrational migration policy to acquire political gains, it seems only fair that countries of origin should use similar contrived policy to secure advantages for their migrants. However such an extreme policy would probably be too obvious a device, and the 'law' would likely be subject to intense lobbying by EEA governments for change once its implications were realised.

I intend to examine a more nuanced example that is intended to offer potential benefits to migrants, countries of origin and countries of
destination. This humane irrational policy would arbitrarily allow free
movement for people over age 50 who live in countries that have a
sizeable migrant population already within the EEA. However, this proposed policy could be implemented according to any geography as long
the mobility benefits are available to everyone over 50. Modern migration often presumes the movement of the young while older people remain behind (NIDI 2001); a consequence of the forced separation of
these generations has a number of consequences and opportunity costs
for the migrant family and the countries of destination and origin
(King & Vullnetari 2006). Young migrants often experience crises in
destination countries and are unable to turn to their elders for support
and help. The often long separations from their families in the country
of origin, because of their new commitments in the destination country, lead to home links becoming tenuous and returns becoming lost
dreams (Castles, Booth et al. 1984):

- Elders being unable to 'grand-parent' means social penalties and
  lost securities as they are often unable to support the younger migrant family members, including the 'policing' of young men and
  supplying important childcare. Reliable childcare releases more women, often including local women, into the labour market with less
  demand on crisis resources.
- Young migrants also lack the support of skilled elders, who can often 'add value' to young labour, particularly in construction, so increasing the employability of both migrants. Those over age 50 are
  not usually infirm; most people are fit and active in their fifties.
  Therefore, very young and vulnerable migrants could be replaced by
  older migrants; waitresses and domestics in their fifties might reduce trafficking opportunities.
- Families with elders are often able to plan more strategically as a
  unit, and there is often better management of care and family crisis, and promotion of investments and savings for the household
  group.
- Care drain: the very elderly are increasingly vulnerable and lonely
  in the country of origin. Solutions for the very elderly are usually
  about migrant return to care or local institutional responses or even
  abandonment. The mobility of the middle-aged allows them to divide their caring between country of origin and destination, as they
  are not trapped in a country of destination by irregular status.
  (Grandmothers are often overstayers as they remain irregularly in a
  destination country to care for grandchildren.)
- Mobile elders maintain transnational social stability and order, and
  they also encourage eventual returns, as older migrants often have

more established home links and investments, so they plan better for returns.

This policy would therefore supposedly encourage the transnational links of migrants by strengthening their families' abilities to extend care and support to one another. Such links could be presented as also encouraging circular migrations, as such families would still be well connected to their country of origin. Some social costs would be reduced because crises would be mitigated and some direct benefits to the country of destination citizens would accrue, such as increased childcare provision available through the new influx of potential child minders. The policy might mitigate against integration, but governments seem to have an understanding that while some migrants will want to settle, many others would only want to be participants in the labour market as long as that participation is predictable and secure. Harris (2005) argues in 'The Royal Society for the Encouragement of Arts, Manufactures & Commerce (RSA) reports on migration and the UK' that there is a need to separate migration streams into those migrants who intend to settle and therefore should 'integrate' and those who are participating in the labour market, do not intend to settle and therefore do not need to fully integrate. It should also be considered that in the case of the NAS migrants there is probably a need for the UK to 'integrate' into a developing European culture rather than the NAS Europeans integrating into a more confined 'British' culture.

It is now openly recognised that many of the NAS migrants are engaged in repeated circular migrations for labour between the NAS and the UK. This circular migration could be the consequence of such migrants having the security of knowing that they have the right of return to the UK (Taylor 2006). Therefore, similar mobility for those over the age of 50 from other communities could increase this desired form of migration among other migrant groups. The erstwhile problem of a lack of integration then becomes a positive indicator of a desire to return to the country of origin. Other problematic issues regarding possible burdens on the healthcare or welfare systems could be the subject of co-development strategies linked to mandatory health insurance and pension arrangements for such migrants, so such problems can certainly be obscured if not resolved.

It is easy to see how a mobility policy for those over age 50, regardless of any evidence to support its beneficial claims, could be represented as:

1. reducing settlement and promoting migrant returns;
2. delaying the initiation migration of many younger potential migrants;
3. preventing crime and trafficking among young migrants;

4. reducing burdens on social services;
5. encouraging investment in the country of origin;
6. supporting the flexibility required in the labour market;
7. transferring European values into important client states;
8. encouraging skilled migrants to stay in the country of origin to acquire experience and skills that will eventually maximise the benefits of later migration;
9. allowing young workers in the country of origin to be promoted, and with such advancement, encouraging them to stay in the country of origin;
10. including other potential benefits for all the stakeholders, especially the migrants.

Such representations are social constructions (Victor 1998) that could easily be reconstructed to represent the proposed policy as dangerous for the following reasons:
1. It mitigates and deters social integration.
2. The policy ignores the current pressures in the country of origin of very large young unemployed populations.
3. It will permit hardened criminals and other social outcasts with weak ties to the country of origin to relocate in the EEA.
4. It will increase the burden on the health service as the middle-aged will quickly become increasing users of health care.
5. Older migrants remit their incomes instead of investing in the host country.
6. Older migrants are not as flexible as younger migrants and are not so willing to accept the dirty, dangerous and demeaning jobs that they are needed to fill.
7. Older migrants will export patriarchal, misogynistic and other alien values into EEA communities, and police these values among young migrants.
8. It will create a substantial brain drain and removed skilled and experienced workers from the country of destination.
9. Various sectors in the country of origin will become dependent on undertrained and underskilled youth.

In understanding the social construction of policy we identify the importance not so much of evidence, but of contrived representation (Victor 1998) and therefore the need of academic researchers interested in influencing policy to take the time to represent humane policy appropriately. Appropriately contrived constructions incidentally supported by evidence might be adopted and implemented. In pandering to the whims of such social constructionist fancies, there is the hope that as an increasingly humane migration regime is institutionalised, the political need to appear tough on migrants will be mitigated.

Migrants acquiring this new mobility for those over the age of 50 would accrue various benefits, the most important probably being the benefit of regular contact with their migrant children and grandchildren. However, other benefits or deficits would become apparent as migrants used the new mobility and investigated its possibilities.

This humane policy would actually have a good fit with the current irrational policymaking of the UK that is intended to project illusions of control and management. This is an example of how an imagined migration policy that fits in with the interests and desires of migrants can be presented in the context of irrational and capricious policymaking as an important measure to control and manage migration. I chose the migrants' desire for the mobility of those over 50 as the subject for my innovative migration proposal because I wanted to demonstrate the ease with which irrational policy can be imagined while also being humane. Furthermore, such imagined policy can also be presented as resolving a migration crisis such as reducing crime among young migrants or increasing the return of labour migrants and as such offers the opportunity for governments to be seen to manage a migration crisis.

In imagining policy, evidence can take second place to pragmatic considerations. Regarding the *Realpolitik*, many senior policymakers are over 50. These policymakers can more easily identify with the subjects of this proposal whom they can presume to be like; they share similar concerns, interests and 'family values', therefore seeming safe to have within the policymakers' own space. The aged migrants are unlike young male migrants who are often considered potentially criminal or politically 'dangerous', or young female migrants who are at risk of either becoming prostitutes or trafficking victims, with these categories there is a perceived need for considerable interventions and control. This policy proposal is therefore based on a notion that this demographic coincidence could be levered into policy on the basis of such intangibles, and should be adapted according to these various illusions and prejudices until a fit is achieved, i.e. participants might be required to produce a police certificate to prove they are not criminals so as to reassure the public that criminals will be excluded. This humane policy was first imagined and then 'evidence' or supposed benefits constructed to support its supposed value. As this is how policy is actually made in the UK, it would seem that by deliberately constructing a proposal that could fit such a process and could be expected to elicit sympathy from policymakers over 50, this proposal demonstrates an innovative *Realpolitik* for developing policy.

Conclusion

In accepting that migration policy is often neither rational nor humane, there is a consequential need to accept that evidence-based policymaking is a rare and exceptional event. Therefore, academics should be able to embrace the irrational and bizarre in supporting the innovative evolution of humane migration policy by indulging in the social construction of imagined policies, for such policies might actually be adopted and implemented. This paper has demonstrated that there is a need for such innovation and thus the production of socially constructed migration policies that are not necessarily dependent on evidence, but are humane policies that policymakers can present as solutions to a perceived migration crisis and as able to quell moral panic regarding migration.

References

Aron, L. (1991), 'The Russians Are Coming: Millions of Soviet Refugees Will Be Fleeing to the West', *The Heritage Foundation Policy Review* 58: 44.

Baldwin-Edwards, M. (2001), 'Semi-Reluctant Hosts: Southern Europe's Ambivalent Response to Immigration', *Mediterranean Migration Observatory Working Papers*. Athens: MMO.

BBC (2005), 'Q&A Foreign marriages rules', BBC Online, 1 February 2005.

BBC (2006), 'Reid outlines new EU work curbs', BBC News Online 24 October 2006.

BBC (2004), 'Beating the sham wedding cheats', London, BBC News Online.

Bobeva, S. (2006), 'Leaving Bulgaria for the UK?', BBC News, Bulgaria 27 September 2006.

Browne, D. (2004), 'Pre-marriage lawful status eligibility requirement for marriages involving non-EEA foreign nationals', Hansard, Column 1381W.

Casciani, D. (2006), 'Sham marriage law breaches rights', London, BBC News Community Affairs.

Castles, S. et al. (1984), *Here for good: Western Europe's new ethnic minorities*. London, Pluto Press.

Clayton, G. (2006), *Are Human Rights and the maintenance of national border ultimately irreconcilable?* Law, Migration and Human Rights: Current Challenges, IDS, Sussex: SCMR, University of Sussex.

Cohen, S. et al. (2002), *From Immigration Controls to Welfare Controls*. London, Routledge.

Crisp, J. & C. Boswell (2004), *Poverty, International Migration and Asylum*. Helsinki: UNV WIDER.

Davies, J. (2005), *Restrictions on the Marriage of Non-EEA citizens in the UK*. T. McNulty and Home Office Minister. London.

Dølvik, J. & L. Eldring (2006), Status Report January 2006: 'The impact of EU Enlargement on labour mobility to the Nordic countries', *Semi-annual memo from a Working Group under the Labour Market Committee of the Nordic*. Oslo: Council of Ministers.

Freire, P. (1970), *Pedagogy of the Oppressed*. New York: Continuum.

Home Office (2005), 'New rules for getting married in the United Kingdom: Questions & Answers', London: Home Office IND.

JCWI (2004), 'Marriage Registrar Campaign', London: Joint Council for the Welfare of Immigrants.

King, R. & J. Vullnetari (2006), 'Orphan pensioners and migration grandparents: the impact of mass migration on older people in rural Albania', *Ageing and Society* 26: 783-816.

NIDI (2001), 'Why do people migrate?', *Statistics in focus, population and social conditions* 3(1).

Reid, J. (2006), 'Romanian and Bulgarian workers', Hansard HC Col. 82WS.

RSAMC (2005), 'Migration: A Welcome Opportunity —, A new way forward by the RSA Migration Commission', London: RSA.

Taylor, L. (2006), 'Changing Pattern of Migration from Poland to the UK', *Thinking Aloud*, UK, BBC Radio 4.

Victor, J. (1998), 'Moral panics and the social construction of deviant behaviour: a theory and application to the case of ritual child abuse', *Sociological Perspectives* Fall.

Webster, P. (2006), 'Reid wins battle over foreign worker quotas', *The Times*, London: 24 October 2006.

Wright, C. (1959), *The Sociological Imagination*. New York: Oxford University Press.

In-country 'refugee' processing arrangements: a humanitarian alternative?

Judith Kumin, UNHCR Brussels[1]

Introduction

The number of asylum applications in industrialised countries has declined steadily in recent years. Within the European Union, applications in 2005 dropped to around 237,000, their lowest level in over a decade and just half the number recorded in 2000.[2] This may in part be explained by improved conditions in certain countries of origin, for instance in Afghanistan. However, it is probably primarily due to measures taken by destination countries to deter movements to their territories. Most of these measures are not implemented at the territorial border but offshore, through visa controls and interception. Although refugees and asylum seekers are often part of broader migratory flows, these deterrent measures do not distinguish between persons seeking protection and other categories of persons on the move.[3] The result is that it is increasingly difficult for refugees and asylum seekers to reach industrialised countries.

Without entering into the much-debated question of whether the international legal obligation of states to respect the principle of *non-refoulement* is engaged when they act extra-territorially to prevent asylum seekers from reaching their soil,[4] it can be argued that there is at least a moral responsibility for states to offset control measures with other means to allow persons in need of protection to find it.[5]

For many years, refugee resettlement provided a way for governments far removed from refugee problems to contribute to sharing the refugee 'burden' with countries of first asylum, while deflecting criticism of deterrent measures and restrictive asylum policies. Yet the resettlement of refugees – that is, the selection of refugees in countries of first asylum and their transfer to new countries of permanent residence – is also coming under criticism. It is varyingly seen as a 'pull' factor which encourages people to leave their country of origin, or as discouraging voluntary repatriation. Other concerns include the potential for fraud and manipulation in the selection of refugees for resettlement, and security problems which resettlement can generate in refugee camps, where the demand for resettlement invariably exceeds the places available.[6]

The 1951 Refugee Convention requires that a person be outside his or her country of origin to qualify as a refugee.[7] But flight is difficult, often dangerous or impossible, and frequently can be effected only through illegal means. It is therefore useful to ask whether programmes to resettle persons in need of protection directly from their countries of origin can offer a viable alternative.[8]

Is this option worth pursuing? Pros and cons

On the positive side, even though the numbers involved in 'orderly departure' or 'in-country' processing arrangements are likely to remain modest, such programmes can provide protection to people who need it, and may avert the need for at least some people to move in irregular and risky ways. In-country processing could also be an important manifestation of responsibility-sharing, if it were to reduce the pressure of spontaneous arrivals on countries in the region of origin, and might even serve to reduce regional tensions.

Like traditional resettlement programmes, in-country processing allows states to manage and control their intake of persons in need of protection. For the beneficiaries, it eliminates the need to spend a period in limbo in a country of first asylum. By definition, in-country processing requires some degree of dialogue between the country of resettlement and the country of origin, and as a result, such programmes may contribute to defusing tense situations, building cooperative relations between states, and promoting basic human rights, including both the right to leave one's country and the right to seek and enjoy asylum from persecution.

On the negative side, in-country processing – even where it is politically feasible – entails a number of problems and potential risks. The principal one is the danger that becomes an 'alibi' for blocking access to asylum. States may be tempted further to impede access to their territory and to their asylum procedures, using the argument that there are legal channels for entry. In addition, an applicant will inevitably be identified to, or identifiable by, the country of origin and therefore may be in danger while the processing is underway, or if he or she is ultimately not accepted for resettlement. Also, the process tends to lack transparency and due process, as visa decisions are discretionary, generally not motivated and usually cannot be appealed. As such, in-country processing (like refugee resettlement) may be perceived as more arbitrary than existing asylum procedures. And finally, in-country processing is likely to benefit only a small number of persons.

Is this option worth pursuing? In the past, such programmes have offered a viable alternative to irregular departures, and have helped to preserve asylum in countries in the region of origin. The most note-worthy example is the Programme for Orderly Departure from Viet-nam, established in May 1979 by a Memorandum of Understanding between UNHCR and the government of the Socialist Republic of Viet-nam.[9] Today, both Canada and the United States devote significant shares of their refugee resettlement intakes to individuals who have not (yet) left their countries of origin. In 2005, refugees admitted di-rectly from their countries of origin (so-called 'Source Countries') con-stituted 16 per cent of resettlement to Canada. About 26 per cent of the US 2005 refugee resettlement programme was from 'in-country' processing.[10]

An example: Canada's Source Country Class

Canada's Source Country Class applies to persons who are still inside their country of origin or of habitual residence[11] as stipulated in the Immigration and Refugee Protection Regulations.[12] The definition re-flects the programme's roots in Canada's 'Latin American Political Pris-oners and Oppressed Persons Class', which began in the 1980s and ap-plied to Chile, El Salvador and Guatemala. At that time Canadian visa officers were literally selecting people from prisons.[13]

According to the Regulations, to be admitted under the Source Country class, a person must reside in a country that has been desig-nated as a 'source country' and that is his or her country of citizenship or habitual residence, and have been determined by a Canadian immi-gration officer to be in need of resettlement for one of the following reasons:

– He or she is seriously and personally affected by civil war or armed conflict in that country.
– He or she is being or has been detained or imprisoned with or with-out charges, or subjected to some other form of penal control, as a direct result of an act committed outside Canada that would, in Ca-nada, be a legitimate expression of freedom of thought or a legiti-mate exercise of civil rights pertaining to dissent or trade union ac-tivity.
– He or she is, by reason of a well-founded fear of persecution for rea-sons of race, religion, nationality, political opinion or membership in a particular social group, unable or, by reason of such fear, un-willing to avail him or herself of the protection of any of his or her countries of nationality or habitual residence.

In determining the countries in which to operate the Source Country Class, the Regulations specify that Canada consults the Department of

Foreign Affairs, the UNHCR, the Provinces and non-governmental organisations with substantial relevant knowledge, and considers:
– where persons are in a refugee-like situation as a result of civil war
   or armed conflict or because their fundamental human rights are
   not respected;
– where Canadian Immigration Officers work or make routine working visits and are able to process applications without jeopardizing
   their own safety, the safety of applicants or the safety of Canadian
   Embassy staff, and where circumstances warrant humanitarian intervention.[14]

In practice, it has proven difficult for the Departments of Foreign Affairs and Immigration to reach agreement on the list, and for this reason there have not been consultations on the Source Country list for
some time. As a result, the list has remained unchanged for several
years. Countries currently on the list are: Colombia, the Democratic
Republic of Congo, El Salvador, Guatemala, Sierra Leone and Sudan.[15]
   In reality, the programme focuses mostly on Colombians. During
2005, of the 1,629 persons resettled directly to Canada from their
countries of origin, fully 1,579 came from Colombia.[16] Nor has the programme been entirely uncontroversial. In 2004 it was alleged that civil
servants of Colombia's national senate were running a scheme that enabled members of Colombia's left-wing guerrilla groups to obtain visas
for Canada under the Source Country Programme.[17]

An example: the US 'in-country' processing arrangement

The US has operated large-scale in-country processing programmes for
many years, as well as 'hybrid' programmes involving the orderly transfer of persons to a third country for transit processing. This was particularly the case for the resettlement of Soviet Jews and Romanians
from the late 1960s onward, as well as for the resettlement of Cu-
bans.[18]
   The US Immigration and Nationality Act permits in-country refugee
determinations 'in such special circumstances as the President after
appropriate consultation may specify.'[19] Although the Statute does not
establish geographical limits for in-country processing, in practice the
annual Presidential Determinations governing the US refugee resettlement programme have done so. The 2005 Presidential Determination[20] allows for the admission through resettlement of up to 70,000
refugees, including directly from their countries of nationality or habitual residence, 'if otherwise qualified', in the case of persons in Viet-
nam, Cuba, the former Soviet Union,[21] as well as 'in exceptional cir-

cumstances, persons identified by a United States Embassy in any location'.[22]

During fiscal year 2005, more than one in four refugees resettled in
the US came directly from his or her country of origin, including persons from Cuba (6,631), the former Soviet Union (5,875) and Vietnam
(1,850). In addition, there were approximately 1,000 persons from Iran,
who were admitted via an orderly departure arrangement involving
transit processing in Austria. Only a handful of people were admitted
from other locations, under the provision which allows US embassies
around the world to identify persons in need of rescue.[23]

These arrangements are not uncontroversial. The risk of in-country
processing being used to justify interdiction and even *refoulement* was
graphically illustrated in the early 1990s, when the US introduced in-
country processing in Haiti and used it to justify the forcible return of
would-be refugees interdicted at sea. Refugee advocates argued energe-
tically against in-country processing in that context, calling it a 'complete sham – a smokescreen for *refoulement*'.[24]

The 'hybrid' arrangement under which the US government conducts
refugee processing of Iranian religious minorities in Vienna has also
entailed difficulties. The Austrian government issues temporary humanitarian visas for applicants – who must obtain Iranian exit visas – to
come to Austria for US resettlement processing. They must be able to
demonstrate a source of support for their stay in Austria. The US government works through a non-governmental agency, the Hebrew Immigrant Aid Society (HIAS), which conducts initial interviews and
guides applicants through the process in Vienna. Over the past five
years the applications of numerous Iranian applicants under this programme have been denied, leaving the candidates stranded in Austria,
and quite obviously displeasing the Austrian government.[25]

Is this an option for Europe?

A 2002 study on the possibility of meeting protective demands outside
state territory, as a complement to extraterritorial migration control,[26]
considered the operation of procedures both in countries of first asylum and in countries of origin. It noted that this practice is still in its
infancy as far as the European Union is concerned, and concluded that
it was premature to assess whether such programmes could offer an alternative to illegal migration for persons seeking Europe's protection.
The authors cautioned strongly against any premature attempts to dis-
mantle existing protection systems in favour of extraterritorial solutions,[27] while recommending that the European Union work toward

consensus on such 'protected entry procedures', with a view toward eventual adoption of a binding instrument in this respect.[28]

From the vantage point of early 2006, this seems more unlikely than ever. Despite a number of reports[29] recommending the establishment of a European Union resettlement programme, there has been little progress in that direction, and refugee resettlement remains a rare feature of European refugee policy. Of the 25 European Union Member States, only Denmark, Finland, Ireland, the Netherlands, Sweden and the United Kingdom operate refugee resettlement programmes. All together these programmes account for only 3 to 5 per cent of all refugees resettled annually worldwide. None of these countries operates an in-country processing arrangement.

The modest recommendation in the European Union's 2004 Hague Programme that Member States participate in the resettlement of refugees in the context of pilot Regional Protection Programmes[30] has met with a muted response from the EU-25.

However, it is worth asking whether European Union countries would respond more positively to suggestions of resettlement directly from countries of origin, rather than from countries of first asylum? To the extent that apprehension of creating 'pull' factors or encouraging fraud are concerns of European governments, in-country processing arrangements might be more attractive, if they could be implemented in a manner consistent with states' relations with the source countries, and with bilateral political interests.

The way forward

Although UNHCR was – with the US government – the architect of the Programme for Orderly Departure from Vietnam, which ultimately enabled hundreds of thousands of Vietnamese to resettle safely,[31] it has never taken a formal position on the issue of in-country processing using refugee resettlement quotas. To the extent that UNHCR has pronounced itself, it has simply expressed the view that there are 'useful lessons' to be drawn from in-country processing, but that such arrangements should not restrict the right to seek asylum abroad.[32]

A more engaged response from UNHCR might encourage further consideration of this option. In particular, UNHCR and governments might want to assess situations in which in-country processing would be warranted, either because safe access to an asylum country that offers effective protection is not possible or because the absorption capacity of neighbouring states is being overstretched. While UNHCR engagement in in-country processing would require a broader view of protection than has traditionally been accepted by the refugee agency, the new responsibilities it has taken on for the protection of internally displaced people might justify such engagement.

At the same time, it will be necessary to judge whether in-country processing is politically possible, in view of relations with the government in question. This will obviously be particularly sensitive in situations where the persecutor is the state. In such cases it will also be important to know whether the security of candidates for resettlement would be put at unacceptable risk, if they were to seek to access in-country processing mechanisms, as well as whether in-country screening could put immigration staff at unacceptable risk.

As UNHCR and states are working to make traditional refugee resettlement a more 'strategic' tool,[33] it might be worthwhile to consider whether in-country processing could also constitute a 'strategic' measure, if it were to reduce the burden on neighbouring states with limited absorptive capacity, provide an alternative to irregular migration, and contribute to reducing political tensions.

In view of the reluctance of most European countries to engage in refugee resettlement in its traditional form, it is fair to ask whether there is any sense in pursuing discussion of in-country processing. However, to the extent that European governments are now considering the establishment of legal migration programmes,[34] it would appear timely to encourage them to consider including a protection dimension in any such arrangements.

Notes

1. The author is UNHCR's Regional Representative in Brussels. This paper reflects her personal opinions, and does not represent the views of UNHCR or of the United Nations.
2. See www.unhcr.org/cgi-bin/texis/vtx/statistics.
3. See UNHCR (2000), 'Interception of Asylum-seekers and Refugees: The International Framework and Recommendations for a Comprehensive Approach', UN Doc. EC/50/SC/CRP.17, 9 June 2000.
4. Lauterpacht, Sir Elihu & Daniel Bethlehem (2003), 'The scope and content of the principle of *non-refoulement*', in Feller, Turk & Nicholson (Eds.), *Refugee Protection in International Law: UNHCR's Global Consultations on International Protection.* Cambridge, 111 at 67.
5. I am not suggesting that 'alternative measures' may be used to justify control measures, or even to justify *refoulement*. On this subject see Note 24.
6. These and other arguments are set out by David A. Martin in 'The United States Refugee Admissions Program: Reforms for a New Era of Refugee Resettlement' (2005). Migration Policy Institute, Washington, D.C., 2-8.
7. 1951 Convention relating to the Status of Refugees, Article 1A.
8. Also called 'source country' programmes (Canada) or 'in-country processing' (US).
9. UN Doc. A/C.3/34/7 (1979). Other examples include various US-Cuba agreements on orderly emigration, the 'third country processing' of Soviet Jews and of Romanians, the rescue of political prisoners from Chile after the overthrow of President Allende, and the resettlement of Ugandan Asians when they were ordered to leave the country by President Idi Amin. Many of these programmes are described in Gil Loescher & John A. Scanlan (1986), *Calculated Kindness: Refugees and America's Half-Open Door 1945-Present,* New York.
10. Source: UNHCR Washington, D.C. The percentage rises to 28 per cent if one includes the 'third-country processing' in Austria of Iranians.
11. See Citizenship and Immigration Canada information at www.cic.gc.ca/english/refugees/resettle-who.html (consulted on 5 March 2006).
12. Government of Canada, Immigration and Refugee Protection Regulations, Paragraph 148, available at http://laws.justice.gc.ca/en/I-2.5/SOR-2002-227/index.html (consulted on 5 March 2006).
13. Kelley, Ninette & Michael Trebilcock (1998), *The Making of the Mosaic: A History of Canadian Immigration Policy,* Toronto: 406-407.
14. Supra, Note 12, Paragraph 148 (2).
15. Citizenship and Immigration Canada, www.cic.gc.ca/english/refugees/resettle-direct.html (consulted 5 March 2006).
16. Source: UNHCR Ottawa.
17. Oakland Ross (2004), 'Canada is conned into taking rebels', *Toronto Star,* 8 September 2004.
18. See Loescher & Scanlan, Supra, Note 9, 88-95 and Wayne S. Smith (1987), *The Closest of Enemies,* New York, 68-100.
19. 8 U.S.C., Section 1101(a)42(B) (2000).
20. Presidential Determination No. 2006-3 of 24 October 2005, Federal Register 70 (210): 1 November 2005 at 65825.
21. Persons from the former Soviet Union must have been citizens or habitual residents of the former USSR before 2 September 1991.
22. Presidential Determination No. 2006-3, Supra, Note 20.
23. Information from UNHCR, Washington, D.C.

24 Frelick, Bill, 'In-Country Refugee Processing of Haitians: The Case Against', *Refuge* 21 (4): 66-72.

25 Shanfield, Dan (2004), 'Relief for Persecuted Religious Minorities from Iran', *Immigration and Refugee Service of America: Refugee Reports*, 25(1) January/February.

26 Noll, Gegor & Jessica Fagerlund (2002), 'Safe Avenues to Asylum? The Actual and Potential Role of EU Diplomatic Representations in Processing Asylum Requests', Danish Centre for Human Rights, Copenhagen.

27 Ibid. 115.

28 Ibid. 119.

29 See e.g. Noll & Fagerlund, Supra, Note 26; Communication from the Commission to the Council and the European Parliament, 'Improving Access to Durable Solutions', COM (2004) 410 final of 4 June 2004.

30 The Hague Programme: 'Strengthening Freedom, Security and Justice in the European Union', Paragraph 1.6.2, OJ C 53, 3.3.2005; European Commission, Communication on Regional Protection Programmes, COM (2005) 388 final, 1.9.2005, Paragraph 6(7).

31 Robinson, W. Courtland (1998), *Terms of Refuge: The Indochinese Refugees and the International Response*, London: 171-174.

32 UNHCR (2000), 'The Interface between International Migration and Asylum', Geneva, November 2000 (Internal Report).

33 See UNHCR, 'Multilateral Framework of Understandings on Resettlement', and 'Convention Plus Core Group on the Strategic Use of Resettlement' at www.unhcr.org (consulted 5 March 2006).

34 See the European Commission's 'Policy Plan on Legal Migration', COM (2005) 699 final of 21 December 2005.

Open borders, close monitoring

Jeroen Doomernik, IMES

Present migration controls and their failings

Obviously, as yet there are no *European* migration and asylum policies, and current policies and practices are manifold between the Member States. Still, not merely for arguments' sake, we can draw as a broad picture two kinds of regimes vis-à-vis uninvited migrants that are prevalent in Europe: the Southern regime of irregular labour migration and the Northern regime of asylum seeking. We should note that the general perception of the (politically) problematic nature of these movements is much less in the first than in the second one. Even though the seriousness of the issues is perceived differently, there is general agreement that restrictive policies are required in order to keep unsolicited migrants at bay. Three types of measures are being employed:

1. physical barriers, natural or man-built, including deployment of border guards;
2. administrative external controls in the form of visa and other documentary requirements and carrier sanctions;
3. internal exclusionary measures aimed at limiting economic, social and other forms of participation.

What governments often hardly address are the causes of irregular migration, neither domestically nor in countries of origin. In the latter we observe a fatal mix of rapid demographic growth, increasing underemployment and unemployment due to economic stagnation and failed or failing states, which together give rise to considerable emigration pressure (Doomernik & Kyle 2004; Neske & Doomernik 2006; Doomernik 2006; GCIM 2005). It is obvious that governments of European states can only intervene directly in the economic or demographic processes taking place elsewhere to a limited extent. That the ability to intervene domestically is also limited – though to a varying extent – is less obvious. Still, economic theories – e.g. segmented and dual labour market theory – allow us to predict a permanent and probably growing demand for informal, low-skilled employment (e.g. Piore 1979; Sassen 1994). In other words, we witness a growing supply of uprooted people willing to migrate to the industrialised nations and within those a considerable demand for them to arrive. To varying extents this demand is not acknowledged by governments of receiving states. Especially under the Northern regime, states find this problematic, as they tend to have considerable numbers of legal residents who are welfare-dependent, and therefore should be employed over newcomers. At the same time, the capacity and willingness to drastically enforce employer sanctions tend to be missing (Martin & Miller 2000). In these states, furthermore, precisely because of generous welfare provisions there is little room for regularisations, and migrants who hope to gain a residence permit, or want to prevent deportation when apprehended, have little alternative but to apply for asylum. Arguably, this perceived need has seriously undermined access to protection for those in real need of it because attempts to curtail the arrival of unsolicited migrants equally, or even more so, affect genuine refugees.

Other effects of progressive attempts to curtail unsolicited migration can be summarised as follows:

1. Defensive measures clearly make entering Europe more difficult but certainly not impossible. They do, however, make migration (much) more expensive. The investments thus required – such as for the services of a smuggler – put migrants in a problematic situation. If they are apprehended, making them return home is virtually impossible as the investment has not paid off; especially since the money involved might not be just the migrant's own but is put up by relatives. This may even lead to a situation in which these relatives have given up part of their own livelihood in return for expected remittances from the migrating relative.

2. Those migrants who cannot afford safe modes of travel run a considerable risk if they opt for the rickety boats that cross the Mediterranean or take people from Western Africa across to the Canary Islands. Being transported concealed in a lorry or aboard a ship is also known to be risky. The NGO United reports the number of known deaths among those who seek to scale the walls of Fortress Europe to be 6,300 since 1993.

3. The Dublin Regulation (Dublin II) should ensure that only one Member State takes responsibility for an asylum request (to curb asylum shopping). This geography-based logic in practice easily leads to asylum seekers and refugees ending up in the 'wrong' country; i.e. not the country they, for practical reasons, would integrate in most easily (through social contacts, cultural affinity or language proficiency), thus causing undue loss of human and financial capital (think of those instances where a refugee faces prolonged unemployed or underemployment and needs state-funded language and other training).

4. The asylum adjudication process in – at least some – EU Member States has been turned into a fast-track procedure with little concern for a fair outcome (*in dubio contra reo* seems to have become the guiding principle). The possibilities to appeal are kept to a minimum so a refugee who is not able to provide a credible story in the very first instance is not given another hearing, not even in another country. In effect, migrants whose interests would be very well served with support from the authorities are denied such, often categorically, and are thus left to fend for themselves. As we saw, return is rarely an option for those whose goal is primarily economic in nature. Nor is it one for those who had good cause to flee for obvious reasons.

In short and with only little exaggeration, we can conclude that migration controls aimed at curbing unsolicited migration do not achieve what they are designed for, but do cause considerable harm to receiving states and migrants alike. And this is happening at enormous financial costs. Martin (2003) estimates that for five industrial countries alone – the US, Canada, Germany, the Netherlands and the UK – the annual cost of patrolling the borders, the enforcement of immigration law and the support of asylum seekers is seventeen billion US dollars. For all the industrialised countries together, this sum must be several times higher. In fact, as Martin adds, when spent on addressing the root causes of uprooting people in the developing part of the world, this might have considerably more impact on reducing irregular migration. Moreover, when policies fail to have the intended effects and instead have perverse outcomes, the consequences in terms of legitimacy of government actions are potentially considerable. This is not least the case when it occurs in such a highly politicised domain as that of migration controls. Also, the corrupting effects of black money earned by human smugglers and other such indirect effects within societies should also not be dismissed.

We also see all over Europe – and again especially under the Northern regime – a tendency to employ instruments from other policy fields, notably that of criminal law enforcement. Assisting migrants with an irregular border crossing has been defined as a (serious) crime during the 1990s, and more detention capacity has been created to detain illegal immigrants until they can be expelled (which often turns out to be impossible for reasons spelled out above). Moreover, irregular residence in itself has been made a criminal offence in a number of countries (Neske & Doomernik 2006). When it comes to irregular migration of women, a tendency can be observed to put that under a general heading of 'trafficking in women' which, on the one hand, again associates this with crime and, on the other, justifies strong measures to combat this type of migration in order to protect women's rights – who then are victims by definition (Kapur 2005). In the public mind, irregular migration has become associated not with people in need, but with abuse, crime and security threats to which states must firmly respond. Once this path has been chosen, turning back becomes politically difficult and risky. All in all, it seems safe to conclude that this process of criminalisation of irregular migration makes it difficult to retain a clear mind when thinking about alternative means of regaining control.

Just and sensible criteria for a migration control system

Which criteria would we expect to be fulfilled by an ideal system for migration management? Two sets of these should probably be addressed: moral and practical ones. For the moral criteria, we might start from the very simple liberal notion that there must be very severe grounds for a justified limitation to an individual's freedom of movement or infringement of his or her liberties, be it a citizen or an alien [for discussions of where this line can or should be drawn, see e.g. Bader (1995) versus Walzer (1995) Carens (1999) versus Mailaender (1999), Harris (1995, 2002), Hayter (2000) or, specifically looking at refugees, see e.g. Gibney (2004)]. Next follows the principle that we should protect people who are subjected to such infringements elsewhere. Such a principle, obviously, has a much wider scope than that of the Geneva Convention but should maybe not, by definition, be as far reaching in its consequences.

In practical terms, migration management should be effective in reaching its aims; it should also be *cost*-effective, i.e. require much lower investments than we currently are seeing. The aims would be to keep out those migrants who seek to do harm (criminals and terrorists); to let in those migrants who economically benefit both themselves and receiving societies; and to protect those migrants or refugees who are in need.

Labour markets and migrants

Most economists would agree that labour migration – when left alone – overall is economically beneficial. If all economic factors can freely move to where they can fulfil their optimal utility – i.e. not only a global free flow of capital as we currently witness but also of labour – states of origin benefit from remittances, the migrants and their households can diversify their sources of income, and it serves as a vital addition to labour markets in receiving countries. In the latter, it particularly serves both demand at the bottom end of the labour market, where it helps preventing structural inflation, and at the top end, where it adds valuable human capital. There are, nevertheless, political reasons that prevent governments of receiving states letting labour migration happen unchecked. However, most of these political reasons may well not be justified. The most powerful and frequently invoked argument is the protection of the native labour force from being crowded out. From an economic point of view this is not necessarily a valid argument. Harris (1995), for instance, convincingly argues that imported labour tends to be complementary to native labour. Others, like Borjas et al. (1996), find only limited evidence for wage-dumping effects and, if those are in evidence, they are small and limited to low-skilled workers (Op. cit., Ottaviano & Peri 2006). Obviously, this is less clear-cut in labour markets that are highly state-regulated – as is typically the case in welfare states – yet we must assume the same principles to be at work. The extent to which these measures (restricting access to the labour market for migrants) in reality serve the interests of the domestic labour force probably is an open question, for we know these states push many workers from the labour market (unemployment benefits, social security, early retirement and such provisions), and it is not at all clear whether this would have been different when migrants would have liberal access to these same markets. In short: I am not convinced that it serves any purpose – other than to lessen fears invoked earlier – to restrict access of immigrants to a labour market.

The need to restrict access is more evident when it comes to welfare provisions. Opening up those to anyone just present on the territory of the welfare state creates the risk of free-riding. Welfare typically is based on two sources: insurance and taxes. As far as the first type is concerned, the need to restrict access (or rather participation) is not given – on the contrary. A worker who suffers an accident should be insured against the damages involved. This makes it essential that all workers are obliged to be insured. Employers are to be made responsible for this, and this is what law enforcement should be targeted at. To prevent employers from dodging this responsibility, they might be held liable – regardless of insurances – in each and every case of a work-related incident.

The second type of welfare provisions usually falls under the heading of social security – the safety net of last resort for those not able to provide for themselves and who have no claim to an insurance-based income – and usually is of an open-ended nature. Access to this type of provision and also to subsidies could, however, be made conditional on and/or proportional to having contributed to the country's tax coffers. Pensions can be tax-based, insurance-based or both. Here too access should be in proportion to contributions. It would seem wise to make this access not dependent on the location where it is enjoyed, so as not to force a migrant to stay in any given country against the interests of all parties involved.

This brief exercise gives us cause to argue that restricting labour migration might not be the necessity we are often lead to believe. As employers will still want to employ migrants and others in an irregular fashion – in order to dodge taxes and premiums – this can be addressed much more efficiently if an employee need not fear deportation and can seek support from the trade unions. Moreover, law enforcement officials can be deployed much more efficiently if conditions of work are their only concern. As Martin and Miller (2000) suggest, employer sanctions at present are not particularly effective because much effort of the authorities goes into enforcing migration law as such. They also suggest that more investment in technology might improve enforcement. Sanctions for employers who might otherwise bend the rules should be serious enough. Fines that take away any profits made from sub-standard employment practices or even ones that are higher would be appropriate. Additionally, those fines could be paid as a premium to the employee (to compensate for damages and as an incentive to report the employer).

Some would argue that such openness would cause many to come and look for a future in Europe. If taking place at all, this effect would soon wear off if the supply of labour substantially exceeds the demand. In the longer run, it would probably create much higher mobility, not just of migrants entering, but also of migrants leaving with the rise and fall of temporary demand for work or, more generally, with the economic cycle. At present, the transaction costs of entering and leaving are such that this mobility is much smaller, which is of no benefit to anyone.

Refugee protection

If we hope to increase our ability to protect those uprooted people who first and foremost need our help, we have taken one important step towards that goal by not forcing migrants with no other claim to legal residence to ask for asylum. This we can do if we, as discussed above, open up our labour market to all newcomers, and further, by unlinking the fact of actual presence on our territory from the issue of (il)legality. The principal rule should then be: unless decided otherwise, all aliens who are in the EU are legally present. When would we see good cause to decide otherwise? If a migrant poses a serious threat, or has more or less seriously broken the rules of our societies, this person is deemed to be an undesirable alien and can (and should) be expelled. In order to make this possible, the focus of control should no longer be our (external) borders – but a comprehensive database. Anyone entering the territory of the EU is free to do so under one condition: being registered in this database. The register contains basic ID and some biometric characteristics to make identification foolproof. Moreover, for people in need of protection, this is the proper moment to make it known if they need financial or other forms of state support. In order to prevent a potential free-rider problem from occurring, failing to file an asylum claim at the moment of first entering the EU makes any future claim inadmissible (although this obviously may be reconsidered in view of future crises abroad). If linked with exclusion from the labour market for a meaningful period of time, this should lead to relatively small numbers of applicants and few attempts at abuse, thus taking considerable strain from the asylum adjudication process. Mirroring German federal practices, a distribution mechanism could be put in place that matches refugee applicants with Member States on the basis of relevant social and human capital criteria and takes burden-sharing principles, which would replace the Dublin mechanism, into consideration.

This database would be a very economic tool for monitoring and controlling migration because it allows the authorities to keep track of migrants and their employment situation. The latter is a vital element because it makes it possible to establish precisely how much access to the welfare state a newcomer has accumulated. The saved resources could be invested in dealing with the root causes of migration – not hoping for short-term effects – on both ends: improving living conditions in countries of origin and controlling conditions of work at home.

Conclusion

In sum: the solution for the mess our asylum and restrictive migration controls has turned into can – in my view – only be found by going into the direction of smaller, less invasive, state intervention and by allowing considerably more self-selection among potential and actual migrants. It is also going to be necessary to put considerably less emphasis on binary choices of the 'either you're in or you're out' type, both on the side of the state and the migrant. It makes static what by its very nature is a highly dynamic process. Moreover, the underlying causes are of a very long-term nature, whereas attempts at interventions tend to be ad hoc and aimed at quick results (see also Penninx & Doomernik 1998).

Solutions in these directions are only feasible if migration can be released from its association with 'problems' and 'threats' to security, the
economy, labour market, etc. In other words, it should return to being
a small political concern. Unfortunately, it seems we are presently
caught in a Catch 22 situation whereby any government admitting to
being nearly impotent in regulating migration commits political suicide. As a result, our policymakers see themselves forced to invest even
more resources in just more of the same – or even stronger – medicine
instead of looking for alternative recipes.

References

Bader, Veit (1995), 'Liberalism and the Order Citizenship and Exclusion: Radical Democracy, Community, and Justice. Or, What Is Wrong with Communitarianism?', *Political Theory* 23 (2): 211-246.

Borjas, George J., Richard B. Freeman & Lawrence F. Katz (1996), *Searching for the effect of immigration on the labor market*, Cambridge, Massachusetts: National Bureau of Economic Research (Working Paper 5454).

Carens, Joseph (1999), 'Reconsidering Open Borders', *International Migration Review* 33 (4): 1082-1097.

Doomernik, Jeroen (2006), 'The Globalisation, Migration and Trafficking Nexus: European Outcomes', in Christien van den Anker & Jeroen Doomernik (Eds.), *Trafficking and Women's Rights*. Houndmills: Palgrave, 201-218.

Doomernik, Jeroen & David J. Kyle (Guest Eds.) (2004), 'Introduction' to Special Issue of the *Journal of International Migration and Integration* 4 (3) on 'Organized Migrant Smuggling and State Control: Conceptual and Policy Challenges': 265-272.

Gibney, Matthew J. (2004), *The Ethics and Politics of Asylum. Liberal Democracy and the Response to Refugees* Cambridge: Cambridge University Press.

Global Commission on International Migration (GCIM) (2005), *Migration in an interconnected world: New directions for action* Geneva: GCIM.

Harris, Nigel (1995), *The New Untouchables. Immigration and the New World Worker*. London/New York: I.B. Tauris.

Harris, Nigel (2002), *Thinking the Unthinkable. The Immigration Myth Exposed*. London/New York: I.B. Tauris.

Hayter, Teresa (2000), *Open Borders. The Case Against Immigration Controls*. London: Pluto Press.

Kapur, Ratna (2005), 'Travel Plans: Border Crossings and the Rights of Transnational Migrants', *Harvard Human Rights Journal* 18 (Spring): 107-138.

Martin, Philip & Mark Miller (2000), *Employer sanctions: French, German, and US experiences*. Geneva: ILO (International Migration Papers No. 36).

Meilaender, Peter C. (1999), Liberalism and Open Borders: The Argument of Joseph Carens', *International Migration Review* 33 (4): 1062-1081.

Neske, Matthias & Jeroen Doomernik (2006), 'Comparing Notes: Perspectives on Human Smuggling in Austria, Germany, Italy and the Netherlands', *International Migration* 44 (4): 39-58.

Ottaviano, Gianmarco I.P. & Giovanni Peri (2006), 'Rethinking the effects of immigration on wages', Cambridge, Massachusetts: National Bureau of Economic Research (Working Paper 12497).

Penninx, Rinus & Jeroen Doomernik (1998), 'Towards migration regulation in globalised societies' in Hans van Amersfoort & Jeroen Doomernik (Eds.), *International Migration. Processes and Interventions* Amsterdam: Het Spinhuis: 129-138.

Piore, Michael P. (1979), *Birds of Passage. Migrant Labour and Industrial Societies* Cambridge: Cambridge University Press.

Sassen, Saskia (1994), *The Mobility of Labor and Capital. A Study in International Investment and Labor Flow*. Cambridge: Cambridge University Press (original 1988).

Walzer, Michael (1995), 'Response to Veit Bader', *Political Theory* 23 (2): 247-249.

The Development Visa Scheme revisited

Michael Jandl, ICMPD

Introduction

The Development Visa (DV) Scheme as an innovative 'Proposal for a Market-based Migration Control Policy' was first presented in a workshop at the International Metropolis Conference 2004 in Geneva.[1] It was not until the publication of a full paper with the same title on the webpage of the Global Commission on International Migration in 2005 that the concept received wider attention and drew significant media coverage. The paper presented here will briefly recapture the main arguments of the DV Scheme and address two commonly made charges against the concept as a policy option. It will then try to identify the main obstacles that work against the adoption of the proposal as an element in current migration policy regimes.

The DV Scheme proposes a market-based scheme for migration control policies that explicitly takes account of economic incentives in formulating individual migration choices. It is based on the European experience with large-scale irregular migration movements, an increasing share of which is mediated through profit-oriented human smuggling activities. The proposal includes a clear set of rules, procedures and sanctions necessary to make this new type of migration control instrument work. After thorough testing and evaluation in a pilot project, the widespread application of the scheme offers the prospect of substantially reducing the demand for human smuggling services and substituting irregular through regular migration flows. A basic characteristic of the proposed DV Scheme is that it is designed to bring substantial benefits to all the important actors in the migration equation – the migrants, the source and the destination countries – but not the human smugglers who stand to lose their illicit income and profits.

The problem: a growing human smuggling industry

While there is much disagreement on the precise magnitude of irregular migration movements to Europe, most observers commonly agree that the role of human smuggling, i.e. the facilitation of illegal entry to states for profit, today accounts for the overwhelming share of illegal entries to European countries.[2]

Before we turn to the presentation of an innovative concept addressing human smuggling as an undesirable phenomenon, let's start with asking a critical question: what is wrong with human smuggling in principle and why should we oppose it? The standard answer to this question seems clear: human smuggling activities have been linked to organised crime, threats to the sovereignty and the internal security of states and the exploitation of human beings in desperate situations.

Addressing the first point, there is little evidence that human smuggling to Europe is controlled by organised crime syndicates or even mafia-like structures.[3] On the contrary, rather than a particular manifestation of organised crime,[4] human smuggling to Europe today looks like a complex service industry, offering a variety of different services (border crossing, accommodation, false or falsified documents, etc.) through a network of suppliers at a range of differentiated prices under market-like conditions.[5] But while the market for human smuggling is not (yet) synonymous with organised crime, it may well become so in the not-so-distant future. As human smuggling is a highly lucrative business, it favours the emergence of criminal networks with high undeclared incomes that can be invested in other criminal activities (e.g. cigarette smuggling).

Turning to the second point, the facilitation of illegal entry against the will of states clearly undermines the management and control of migration movements and, hence, the prerogative of states to determine who can and cannot enter their territories. This, in turn, furthers public perceptions of a 'loss of control' over general immigration flows, which often adds fuel to the growth of xenophobic and populist parties and further restricts room for rational immigration policies. Indirectly, therefore, human smuggling can even have negative consequences for the absorptive and integration capacity of states.

Finally, turning to the third point, human smuggling does not automatically lead to exploitation of the smuggled migrants (in contrast to trafficking in human beings). Nevertheless, and quite apart from the desired effect of being helped to their desired destination, it can have clearly negative consequences for the smuggled migrants themselves. First, there are the hardships and physical dangers that migrants are frequently exposed to by unscrupulous smugglers as evidenced by hundreds of registered (and probably many more unregistered) deaths of irregular migrants annually. Second, the need to engage human smugglers for their journey represents an enormous loss of time and money for the migrants. Typical smuggling fees from an Eastern European country to Western Europe can easily amount to € 4,000, while the smuggling fees from more distant countries like Afghanistan and India can exceed € 8,000 and more. Moreover, in many cases, the journeys of smuggled migrants often take many months and even years. And third, beyond the individual expenses for smuggling services, the income of human smugglers (amounting to several billion euros annually) represent a formidable drain on already scarce resources for development in (usually very poor) source countries.

What the DV Scheme is meant to achieve and what not

The DV Scheme starts from the assumption that irregular migration and human smuggling should be curtailed, and it proposes a scheme that should achieve that aim. It does not attempt to reduce migration in general (i.e. the sum of legal and illegal migration). After all, the demographic logic in Europe clearly indicates a large, unfilled potential for additional immigration over the next decades. Rather, it proposes an innovative approach for 'substituting' the irregular part of migration by regular, authorised migration. Such a 'substitution' effect is more difficult to achieve than appears at first sight. Contrary to popular assumptions, there is no evidence that a simple expansion of legal immigration opportunities would lead to a decrease of illegal immigration. In fact, the opposite may be the case, indicating the importance of migration networks in legal and illegal migration processes.[6] In contrast, the DV Scheme proposes a particular set of economic incentives that would contribute to a decrease in illegal migration through the expansion of legal migration opportunities by way of so-called Development Visas.

The rules of the game

The basis of the proposed Development Visa (DV) scheme is contained in a simple rule: 'Sell legal entry permits to any eligible would-be migrant at roughly the price of currently prevailing smuggling fees! The legal entry permits thus obtained shall be called Development Visas.' This straightforward DV rule needs several qualifications and explanations in order to become operational.

First, the DV Scheme is not exclusive. Thus, this system can run in parallel to current visa and entry permit systems that countries already have. Thus, states can continue to issue 'free' visas to anybody they deem entitled to receive such a visa for specific purposes (e.g. tourists, students, migrant workers, etc.). Anybody who cannot obtain such a 'free' visa can apply for a DV and, if he or she is not specifically excluded from the scheme (see below), will normally be issued a DV upon payment of the set price. An important condition for the system to work, however, is a strict control of current visa-issuing practices as well as enhanced control of the issuing of DVs in order to prevent circumvention and corruption of the scheme.[7]

Second, all applicants for DVs will be fingerprinted and will be excluded from future participation in the scheme in case they violate the rules of the regime. Possible contraventions to the rules may consist of an illegal migration record (thus the need to compare fingerprints with existing databases of apprehended illegal migrants in Europe), overstaying the time period of their DVs without authorisation or other, yet to be defined contraventions to laws and regulations. In short, all applicants are eligible to participate in the DV Scheme, unless they are explicitly excluded from it.

Third, the DV is an all-purpose visa. It gives the right to work in the host country (i.e. in case the migrant can find legal work in the host country, subject to national rules and regulations, she or he is not subject to any additional numerical quotas) or simply to reside in the host country. The DV is not strictly tied to the labour market of the host country, but national labour market services may be called upon to help DV holders to find legal work. In case the migrant is apprehended for carrying out irregular work (i.e. not paying taxes and social security contributions), she or he may be expelled according to current rules and readmission procedures and loses the right to further participation in the DV Scheme.

Fourth, the number of DVs to be issued in any country per year is subject to a numerical quota. This quota should be set high enough to accommodate the projected demand for DVs. At this point it is important to note that the demand for DVs will not be unlimited. In fact, the demand for DVs in any country should be of a similar magnitude as the current demand for smuggling services, as the prices for the two will be roughly the same. Based on a thorough survey of the current volume and structure of human smuggling activities in the country in question, a rough projection of the expected demand, at current smuggling prices, can be drawn up and translated into an annual numerical quota for the DVs.

Fifth, the DVs will be issued for only one host country in which they are valid. Thus, there is a need to coordinate both the total DV quota for any sending country and the individual sub-quotas for host countries across all EU countries (or at least all Schengen countries). Country quotas, sub-quotas and prices will be set annually by the EU Council of Justice, Liberty and Security Ministers (JLS Council). There is also the possibility of charging slightly different prices for DVs for individual host countries.

Tripartion of DV fees

Applicants for DVs have to pay a one-time, non-refundable administrative fee upon applying for participation at the DV office. Once it has been determined that the applicant is eligible (i.e. not excluded from the scheme; see above) and the annual quota is not yet exhausted, the full amount of the DV visa fee is to be paid as an up-front payment. Upon receipt of the payment, the DV is issued and the DV fee is put into a caretakers' account. Thereupon, the DV fee for each DV holder is divided into three equal parts:

One-third will go to targeted development programmes in the sending country, supervised by an appropriately selected development agency. Another third will be reimbursed by the DV office to the DV holder in person upon the return of the migrant within the specified time limit of the DV. Should DV holders not return in time (either because they overstayed the time period of their DVs or because they seized the opportunity to gain another legal residence status in their host country, e.g. through marriage or a work-related stay permit) they will lose this part of the DV fee. Finally, one-third will go to the DV Social Security Deposit (DVSSD) as explained below.

The DV Social Security Deposit (DVSSD)

The DVSSD is designed to cover basic health and welfare expenditure of the host country on behalf of the migrant, should the need for such expenditure arise. It is an insurance scheme administered by the state and is meant to cover expenses for those services only which are normally accorded to any person in need (e.g. emergency hospital treatment, basic welfare services but not expensive treatment of chronic illnesses).

The DVSSD is designed as a contingently mandatory social security scheme. This is to say, the DVSSD will only be drawn upon in case the migrant is not covered through the payment of social security contributions through declared income. If, however, the migrant does assume legal work and does pay regular social security contributions deducted from her or his declared income, that part of the DVSSD where other social security coverage exists will be refunded.[8] Thus, DV holders have a clear economic incentive to decline irregular work offers and seek regular, declared work opportunities instead.[9]

Continuous adaptation and DV pilot project

A basic characteristic of the proposed DV Scheme is that it is designed to bring substantial benefits to all the important actors in the migration equation – the migrants, the source and the destination countries – but not the human smugglers who stand to lose their illicit income and profits. It is therefore to be expected that the implementation of the scheme will bring about some response on the part of the human smugglers in reaction to the changed circumstances. Such reactions might consist in aggressively cutting prices or in increasing marketing efforts to woo new clients. As in many other areas of migration policy, fundamental policy changes will bring about predictable results, as well as unforeseen and unintended consequences. There is thus a need to tailor the DV Scheme to the prevailing local circumstances and then to continuously adapt the DV rules, fees and quotas to the expected and unexpected changes in the policy environment.

To gain the necessary experience for setting up a proper DV Scheme, the mechanisms at work should first be tested in a smaller-scale DV pilot project. Possible candidates for the pilot project could be any small or medium-sized Eastern European country close to the EU, which is currently a significant source country of smuggled migrants, such as Albania or Moldova.

Objections to the DV Scheme

Ever since its presentation, a number of objections have been pointed out by critical reviewers of the DV Scheme. Some of these have already been addressed in the original paper, two more should be taken up here. What appears to be perhaps the most serious objection to the proposed scheme is the possibility of a large excess demand for DV visas (in economic jargon: the demand curve for legal entry might be vastly different from the demand curve for illegal entry, i.e. much higher). If this is the case, then we have a problem: if we set the price of a DV according to this higher demand curve, the DV would be too expensive for the people who now use smugglers. But if we set the price low enough to compete with smugglers, we would attract lots of extra demand from law-abiding people who fancy spending a couple of years in a high-wage labour market, but who would never countenance paying a people smuggler, simply because it is illegal to do so.

To put it differently, how do we make legal opportunities attractive enough to defeat illegal ones on the market, while not facing unrestricted supply? We put a price on it. In addition, to calm fears of the electorate and politicians, we also put a realistic numerical cap on it.

Thus, total migration will be limited by the DV quotas fixed for each year in advance by the host countries. Furthermore, the DV would be restricted time-wise, say to one year (or two or whatever), which means that people would start to calculate how much they are likely to make during that year (or period) and compare it with the price. People may still prefer the smugglers then, but they would then face the risk of apprehension and expulsion long before that year (or period) is over. On the other hand, given the cap and the price, more people may want to use legal opportunities through the DV Scheme than available at the time. However, if this is the case, people may want to wait for a while and try to get into the next year's quota. Meanwhile, policy will have to react on the experience with the first year – set new prices, new quotas, new time periods for the DV based on demand, effective return to home countries and so on.

In reality, of course, we cannot know the 'true' demand curves for legal and illegal migration opportunities *ex ante*. Surveys on the intention to migrate under alternative regimes may help but, in effect, they will reflect intentions rather than future actions. Ultimately we will have to learn about the 'true' demand curves through experience with a smaller pilot project. Based on this experience, the precise parameters of the DV Scheme will have to be carefully calibrated and adjusted year-on-year. For example, if there is a large unmet demand for DVs, states may decide to place existing labour migration arrangements under the DV Scheme (thus bringing in already legal 'free' migration opportunities under the DV Scheme) and raise quotas accordingly.

A second objection that should be briefly addressed here concerns refugees and asylum seekers. It has been pointed out that the proposed scheme does not address the question of access to international protection for those in need of it. This is true only insofar as the issue is not explicitly dealt with in the original proposal. However, without taking a definite stance on the issue, it should be pointed out that asylum seekers could be accommodated in the DV Scheme in several ways. One option would be to exclude DV holders from access to regular asylum procedures, as it could be argued that they do not need access to asylum under their DV status. A second option would be to grant this access and combine it with the economic incentives of the DV Scheme. Should their asylum claim be accepted, they would receive a full refund of the total DV fee plus an integration assistance as a 'start-up package' in their host country. Should their asylum claim be rejected, however, they would have to return immediately and lose all, or parts of, their DV fee as compensation for the administrative costs incurred by the host country. In any case, the very set-up of the DV Scheme will restrict its geographical application, as it requires the full co-operation of the source country in its implementation (for carrying out the development projects financed under the scheme, administering the read-mission of deviating migrants, etc.). Thus, failed states or states sys-tematically violating the human rights of its population will not qualify from the very beginning.

With this important restriction on the type of countries that can qua-lify for participation in the DV Scheme, we can now briefly deal with a third objection that has been made to the proposed scheme: as sending migrants abroad through the DV Scheme will presumably be very at-tractive to many potential sending state governments, the question arises as to whether this would lead to unintended incentives for 'push-ing' their own nationals into the scheme and out of the country. As this could indeed be the case for certain types of governments, it will be im-portant to keep full participation in the DV Scheme contingent on keeping with principles of 'good governance', and restrict the flow of funds raised through the DV fee for development projects in the coun-try of origin in case of misbehaviour. Moreover, as countries have to qualify periodically for further participation in the DV Scheme, compe-tition between states should provide further incentives for full coopera-tion with the DV implementing agency.

Conclusion

The DV Scheme proposes a market-based scheme for migration con-trol policies that explicitly takes account of economic incentives in for-mulating individual migration choices. In this, the proposed scheme differs from most other policies designed to counter irregular migra-tion and human smuggling. Whereas the DV Scheme does not raise the claim to bring about the total elimination of illegal migration and human smuggling activities (as it clearly will not), the scheme could make significant inroads into the reduction of human smuggling activ-ities. And while it is unlikely that a perfect once-and-for-all solution for current and future migration problems will ever exist, it is suggested that the proposed DV Scheme would represent a significant improve-ment – or second-best solution – to current challenges posed by irregu-lar migration.

Notes

1   Michael Jandl is Senior Research Officer at the International Centre for Migration Policy Development (ICMPD). This article is based on a longer version of the original proposal. For details of the scheme, see Jandl, M. (2005), 'The Development Visa Scheme. A Proposal for a Market-based Migration Control Policy', *Global Migration Perspectives* No. 36 (www.gcim.org/en/ir_gmp.html). The views expressed in this article, as well as in the original paper, are those of the author only, and not those of ICMPD as a Vienna-based intergovernmental organization or of its member states.

2   It should be noted that the DV Scheme as a policy proposal was elaborated with a view to counter irregular migration and human smuggling activities and not the problem of trafficking in human beings *per se*, although it is likely to have a mitigating effect on the latter as well. For conceptual, legal and practical reasons, however, it is important to distinguish the two phenomena of smuggling and trafficking. To generalise, the latter always involves an element of exploitation, while the former does not necessarily do so.

3   See Heckmann, F. (2003), 'Mafiastrukturen? Organisierungsformen von Menschenschmuggel', in *Migration, Flüchtlinge und Integration*. Nürnberg: (Schriftenreihe des Bundesamtes für die Anerkennung ausländischer Flüchtlinge) Bd. 11, 138-153.

4   James Finckenauer has argued that human smuggling can be characterised as a 'crime that is organised' rather than as 'organised crime'. See Finckenauer, J.O. (2001), 'Russian Transnational Organized Crime and Human Trafficking', in Kyle, D. & R. Koslowski (Eds.), *Global Human Smuggling: comparative perspectives*, 166ff. Baltimore: The Johns Hopkins University Press.

5   For a theoretical and empirical elaboration of this point see: Bilger, V., M. Hofmann & M. Jandl, (forthcoming 2006), 'Human Smuggling as a Transnational Service Industry. Evidence from Austria', in *International Migration, Special Edition on Human Smuggling*.

6   For an overview of the arguments and statistical evidence, see Jandl, M. & A. Kraler, (2006), 'Links Between Legal and Illegal Migration', in Poulain, M., N. Perrin. & A. Singleton (Eds.), *THESIM – Towards Harmonized European Statistics on International Migration*, 337-371. UCL Presses, Louvain-La-Neuve.

7   Safeguards against fraud would be facilitated by the use of modern technologies, such as the European Visa Information System (VIS) and biometric passports.

8   Thus, for example, when the migrant pays regular social security contributions deducted from regular income for half of the time of the DV validity, he or she will get half of the DVSSD refunded upon return.

9   This could be reinforced by the right of DV holders to sue their employers for the forgone DVSSD upon return to their home country in the case that they were employed undeclared.

References

Bilger, V., M. Hofmann & M. Jandl, (forthcoming 2006). 'Human Smuggling as a Transnational Service Industry. Evidence from Austria.' In *International Migration*, Special Edition on Human Smuggling.

Council of the European Union (2002). 'Council framework Decision of 28 November 2002 on the strengthening of the penal framework to prevent the facilitation of unauthorised entry, transit and residence.' JHA (2002) 946, available at http://europa.eu.int/eur-lex/pri/en/oj/dat/2002/l_328/l_32820021205en00010003.pdf (5 November 2004).

Finckenauer, J.O. (2001). 'Russian Transnational Organized Crime and Human Trafficking.' In D. Kyle & R. Koslowski (Eds.). *Global Human Smuggling: Comparative Perspectives*, 166ff. Baltimore: The Johns Hopkins University Press.

Jandl, M. & A. Kraler (2006). 'Links Between Legal and Illegal Migration.' In M. Poulain, N. Perrin & A. Singleton (Eds.), *THESIM – Towards Harmonized European Statistics on International Migration*, 337-371. UCL Presses: Louvain-La-Neuve.

Heckmann, F. (2003). 'Mafiastrukturen? Organisierungsformen von Menschenschmuggel.' In *Migration, Flüchtlinge und Integration*, 138-153. Nürnberg: Schriftenreihe des Bundesamtes für die Anerkennung ausländischer Flüchtlinge, Bd. 11.

United Nations, (2000). 'Protocol against the Smuggling of Migrants by Land, Sea and Air, Supplementing the United Nations Convention against Transnational Organized Crime.' available at www.uncjin.org/Documents/Conventions/dcatoc/final_documents_2/index.htm (24 March 2004).

Pricing entrance fees for migrants

Holger Kolb[1], IMIS

A realistic liberal economic approach

Although economics has not been among the core disciplines in migration research for quite some time,[2] recently liberal economists have become increasingly active in the discussion about a sustainable and efficient migration policy. The utilisation of the market mechanism for migration policy provides the core of their conceptualisation. This means, in a nutshell, that – departing from the assumption of an existing immigration market – immigration rights should be made tradable and that a price should be charged for the scarcely issued immigration and residence permits. Proponents of such a liberal approach are Becker (1992, 1996) and Straubhaar (2000). All free traders in the first instance would suggest that any immigration restriction[3] causes market distortions and thus should be avoided (Freeman 1995; Hillman 1994). This, however, does not seem to be sensible even for liberals. The reason for the impracticality of the free international movement of people is the fact that most nation-states are welfare states that may function as magnets for immigrants. Unregulated immigration may undermine the welfare state's capability of service. In particular, tax-financed social aid and other benefits, which constitute the margin of subsistence and which are paid independently from previous payments, may operate as a magnet for certain groups of immigrants (Borjas 1999). It is therefore in the self-interest of a state to restrict immigration for those groups (Straubhaar 2002: 84). In other words, welfare states, which aim at providing internal equality, must maintain an external 'threshold of inequality' (Stichweh 1998: 49-61). Realistic market-economy approaches take this structural necessity into account and take leave from advocating generally open borders.

Becker as well as Straubhaar belong to this group of realistic liberals. Their proposals maintain immigration restrictions, but in a market economy and not in a central planning way. All these realistic market economy concepts for migration policy face the same basic problem, namely, that one authority is responsible for deciding on either the price that potential migrants are charged for the right to immigrate or on the quantity of permits to be issued. Straubhaar favours the latter approach and proposes a quota that is allocated by an auction process. One basic disadvantage of this proposal, however, is that the maximum quota must be decided in advance on the political level. Becker's proposal is the opposite of Straubhaar's. He proposes to charge a fixed price for the right to immigrate without the presence of a maximum quota. Although the setting of an entrance fee unrelated to market factors structurally faces the same problems as the political definition of a quota, Becker's proposal seems to be easier to handle because of the presence of various indicators as to the right price. Consequently, every applicant willing to pay the price and subject to a few prerequisites, such as not having a terrorist background, a criminal record or a contagious disease, would be accepted.

Current immigration regimes can be assumed to be neither effective nor efficient. Effectiveness understood as a high degree of goal realisation requires the allocation of those migrants to a particular state that the respective state is in need of. Efficiency postulates a minimum possible utilisation of resources for goal achievement. Labour shortages in different sectors across countries and a huge and chronically overloaded immigration bureaucracy, such as the US Citizenship and Immigration Services, indicate that current immigration policies in all immigration countries are far from satisfying the criteria of effectiveness and efficiency. The present immigration socialism in many immigration countries displays the features that are well-known from socialist and central planning societies: misallocations, oversized bureaucracies and suboptimal service. The main achievement of a market-economy approach on immigration would be the abatement of this lack of effectiveness and efficiency.

The former would be met automatically, because a market-based system capitalises on the infinite knowledge possessed by each individual actor. The immigrants who are willing to pay the demanded entrance fee would automatically have various characteristics that destination countries seek in their entrants. This mechanism can be easily understood by remembering the core assumptions of Becker's work. Gary Becker became famous for his rigorous analysis of the economic approach to all human behaviour.[4] This economic approach is characterised by assuming rationally acting individuals,[5] the importance of equilibrium and stable preferences. Particularly the first assumption explains the smooth and self-controlled allocation mechanism of the entrance fee. The migration process can be understood as an investment decision.[6] Individuals will decide to immigrate in a particular country, anticipating more to receive than to invest. The total amount to be invested in this case amounts to the entrance fee plus other transaction and adjustment costs. Correspondingly, only those individuals would seek entrance who expect a return from the residence permit which exceeds the total costs.

As a result, individuals striving for entrance would have a favourable age profile, since young adults would gain more from migrating because they would receive higher earnings over a relatively longer time period. Furthermore, they would be rather skilled, high-earning and ambitious to afford the entrance fee. In general, it can be assumed that the introduction of a market-based system would induce a positive self-selection of immigrants. In addition to an increased effectiveness, efficiency is assumed to be improved because the entrance fee system does not require points systems, lengthy hearings and a huge immigration bureaucracy. The necessary organisational infrastructure would just require a small public authority which screens for a terrorist background and criminal records and checks the receipt of the money.

Curbing illegal migration through market mechanisms

Furthermore, the entrance fee model can be assumed to have major implications on illegal migration flows which attracted the wider public's attention after the tragic events in Ceuta and Melilla. Illegal migration points out an unavoidable paradox, which states are trapped in. States cannot renounce the management of migration by controlling access to, and stay on, their territory. In doing this they produce the conditions for illegal migration and its dynamics as unintended consequences and a kind of flipside to their control efforts. There seems to be no easy way out of this constellation: neither comprehensive control of migration is possible nor its abolishment. It seems that states can only prepare themselves and make themselves at home with illegal migration being a problem they have to handle without assuming that there is a final solution (Bommes 2006). Understanding migration control efforts and the emergence of illegal migration as 'communicating tubes' which influence each other can clarify the impact of the reintroduction of a legal entrance scheme on illegal attempts to immigrate.

There are quite some indices to suggest that the introduction of a legal, strictly market economy-based system would significantly reduce attempts at illegal entrance, because generally immigrants can be assumed to prefer the legal and safe way to immigrate to a country.[7] The fact that only solvent individuals are granted access to the country is irrelevant in this context, because this also applies to illegal migration. Reliable estimations of the prices charged by human smugglers, who organise the dangerous, time-consuming and often fatal trips to the destination countries, sums up to $ 5,000 for the destination Europe or $ 45,000 for the US (Petros 2005). Therefore, it must be assumed that illegal migrants, who mandate human smugglers to organise the illegal entry trip to Europe or the US, face liquidity problems in a similar way as legal migrants under the conditions of the entrance fee system (Bilger, Hofmann & Jandl 2005: 12). Estimations of the total price for being smuggled to a particular country are fraught with a lot of difficulties. Even assuming that the entrance fee to be fixed by the state[8] may exceed the prices of the smuggling service providers, immigrants opting for the legal way are still much better off even in financial terms.

In addition to the comparison of the entrance fee and the smuggling fee, any individual calculation of the costs of the respective alternatives of immigration also must take into consideration the depreciation costs on the human capital of the immigrants, which arise from the time-consuming smuggling processes, and the constraints illegals face due to their illegality.[9] A precise comparison of the available alternatives to enter a particular country, which considers not only the direct, but also the indirect, costs of the respective alternatives, indicates that in monetary terms the legal way with high probability might be the more attractive option.

In addition to that, the repayment circumstances are much more favourable for legal immigrants. Contrary to immigrants who buy the permission to immigrate by simply paying the entrance fee and in case of liquidity problems can take out a loan from a bank,[10] employer or relatives already living in the destination country, illegal migrants who are not able to pay the full price to the smugglers are exposed to criminal and violent gangs who act as debt collecting agencies for the smugglers. The introduction of an easy and transparent legal way of immigration, therefore, may help to put human smugglers out of business and should prove to be a very effective way to combat human smuggling.

Markets and state regulation

The entrance fee system sounds easy and straightforward, and indeed, it is a major step towards simplification and transparency compared to the complicated immigration bureaucracy. Nevertheless, the entrance fee system induces several minor problems. As already indicated above, this very market-based system is not without any state guidelines and requires the setting of the entrance fee by a political decision. Practically, however, this problem seems to be easily solvable because of various available indicators for the right price. The charged price correlates positively with the amount of welfare benefits.[11] Since it is possible to calculate the average welfare benefits utilisation in different states, the price would be aligned to this amount and would thus automatically result in the acceptance of an optimal number of immigrants.

A second problem is related to the immigration of family members. As the right to found a family is one of the core features of modern society, the entrance fee system must find a feasible solution concerning entry and residence of the family members of an immigrant. In this context it would be possible to charge the entrance fee per family or to grade the fee on a diminishing scale. Furthermore, it must be taken into consideration that some migrants just aspire to a temporary residence permit. Any entrance fee system, therefore, must contain regulations concerning the pay-back conditions of the entrance fee for temporary stayers. Persons who have paid the fee and leave the country again after a certain period of time must be paid back a part of the sum. Presumably, a graded payback related to the length of stay seems to be appropriate.

In order to prevent misunderstandings, it should be noted that the introduction of an entrance fee-based system would result in a major reform of the current labour immigration system, but would not affect asylum and refugee migration regulations. In this respect, regulations concerning asylum and refugee migration would have to complement the entrance fee-based system. Systematically, asylum regulations can be understood as a special 'repair mechanism' to respond to the breakdown of a territorially based system of universal inclusion, in the form of states' expulsion or persecution of their members (Bommes 1999).[12] Straubhaar (2003) uses the metaphor of a house with two separate entrances to illustrate a possibly more efficient immigration regime without violating the humanitarian requirements of liberal democracies. This house consists of two entrances, one main door and a side door. Both entrances lead to separate rooms which are not connected by any alleyway. The main door as the entrance for labour migrants could be regulated according to the proposed entrance fee system. The side door which allows entry and temporary residence for persons in need of protection illustrates the asylum system. Permanent residence, however, is only possible after having entered the country by the main door.[13]

With regards to the practical obstacles, one has to be aware of the fact that the implementation of an entrance fee system to organise immigration is highly unlikely.[14] This is due to a general, rather bad image of market-based solutions and the application of the price mechanism in many different realms of life. Frey (1990: 139-161) analysed the reasons for this bad image and identified four possible explanations: inadequate information, lack of fairness of prices, unwanted distributional effects and destructive effects on morality. This general objection to the price mechanism might even be aggravated in a highly politicised and emotional policy field like migration policy. The proposal of a conversion of immigration policies to the proposed market economy principles by any political group would therefore equal their political suicide. Selling the right to immigrate would probably be perceived as immoral by the majority of the population, although many immigration systems have integrated elements of selling the right to immigrate already for quite a while. The US grants so-called 'employment creation' residence permits to foreign investors who invest at least $ 500,000 and create ten jobs (Hermann & Hunger 2003: 88). In a similar way, the new German immigration act attracts foreign entrepreneurs. On condition of a superordinate economic interest of Germany in the immigration of the respective entrepreneur, which is operationalised as a minimum investment sum of one million euros and the creation of at least ten new jobs, the immigration act grants a residence permit for three years which can be transformed into a permanent permit in case of business success. Many immigration regulations contain these rather complicated and indirect procedures of selling the right to settle. Thus, the conversion to a simpler and more radical immigration regime would not even be a completely new way of organising immigration.

Further to the bad image of market-based solutions, it is widely known that it is in most cases rather naive to follow the self-description of the political system and to take on the description of bureaucrats and politicians as benevolent policymakers (Downs 1957; Niskanen 1971). Interpreting politicians and bureaucrats instead as voter, power and/or budget maximisers, the very small implementation possibilities of the entrance fee proposal become apparent. It is rather inconceivable that politicians and bureaucrats will approve a policy measure which curtails their power and budget or would lead – for the immigration services – to a complete winding up. The proposal of a radical system which mainly relies on the market mechanism induces opposition of influential bureaucratic and political actors that hold the power to impede those regulations.

Conclusion

Recapitulating and parting from the assumption of a certain discontent with the present immigration regulations in most countries, it becomes apparent that mainly human smugglers are the ones who are made worse off compared to the present system. The destination countries would belong to the profiteers because of the additional fiscal revenues and the assumed decrease of illegal migrants. The same would apply to the group of potential immigrants for whom in the case of in-

troducing such a scheme a legal option of entry, which in most cases
might be preferred to the illegal and often life-threatening attempts to
enter illegally, is offered. Nevertheless, despite the various advantages
the introduction of such a scheme will remain unlikely. The desperate
question of Stiglitz (1998: 5): 'why is it so difficult to implement even
Pareto improvements?'[15] remains valid.

Notes

1   I am indebted to the participants who gave their helpful comments at the Innovative
    Concepts for Alternative Migration Policies Workshop at the ICMPD in Vienna.
2   Empirical evidence for this assumption is provided by the National Survey of Immi-
    gration Scholars (NASIS) which was conducted at the end of the 1990s in the US.
    The main aim of NASIS was the assessment of the academic and social background
    of those academics who perceived migration research themselves as sociologists, 28
    per cent as historians, 12 per cent as anthropologists and only 9 per cent as econo-
    mists or political scientists. See Rumbaut (1999: 1285-1301).
3   Migration in an economic view is understood as a function of mobility costs and wel-
    fare differentials (Pies 1995: 151), and thus a phenomenon of arbitrage which contri-
    butes to the correction of market imperfections. In this view, migration should be
    generally approved by states because it contributes to increased economic efficiency
    (Straubhaar 2002: 52-53).
4   Becker was awarded the Nobel Prize for Economics in 1992 for 'having extended the
    domain of microeconomic analysis to a wide range of human behaviour and interac-
    tion, including nonmarket behaviour'. For an excellent review of Becker's work see
    Pies (1998).
5   The assumption of rationally acting individuals is a source of major misunderstand-
    ings. A widespread critique of rational choice approaches concentrates on the as-
    sumption of rationally acting individuals, arguing that rational action, complete infor-
    mation and infinite speed of adoption are empirically rather unlikely. The assump-
    tion of rationality in this context, however, must not be mixed up with the statement
    of rational human beings in an empirical sense. The assumption of rationality must
    not be understood as a falsifiable hypothesis. Rationality in this context must be un-
    derstood as a heuristic device, as a pre-empirical hypothesis which can be used for
    deriving empirical data.
6   See also the early work of Sjastaad (1962: 83), who argues that migration must be
    understood 'as an investment increasing the productivity of human resources, an in-
    vestment which has cost and which also renders returns'.
7   Bilger, Hofmann and Jandl (2005) indicate that the choices for illegal migrants – in
    contrary to legal ones who simply pay the entrance fee of a respective country – to
    opt for their favourite country of destination are rather limited, and that many illegal
    migrants are smuggled to a country which actually was not their first choice.
8   Becker and Becker (1996) propose an entrance fee of $ 50,000 which is well above
    the average smuggling fee.
9   Examples of these constraints are limited job opportunities in the shadow economy,
    as well as limited training and career development opportunities.
10 In a similar way that private banks deal in credits for students who lack the sufficient
    liquidity to pay the tuition fees, banks can issue a credit to immigrants to pay the en-
    trance fee.
11 The proposal by Jeroen Doomernik (2006) 'Open Borders, Close Monitoring', which
    in the first instance sounds quite naive, goes in the same direction. Doomernik in-
    deed argues for open borders and the abolishment of border controls. The described
    magnet effects of welfare states and a resulting excessive demand of welfare state
    provisions, however, are circumvented in the proposal by granting welfare provisions
    depending on the duration of stay. Immigrants are thus partially excluded from re-
    ceiving welfare benefits. This exclusion reduces the magnet effect. Problems, how-
    ever, might occur in the case of certain welfare state provisions and collective goods
    which lack the necessary excludability. For them, the magnet effect persists.

12   This universalism of inclusion can be attributed to the organisational principles of the political system. As the world population is distributed into nation-states, state membership is immediate and, in most cases, permanent and exclusive. Every individual must be a member somewhere. In case of the violation of the universalism of inclusion by dictatorial states, the international asylum system organises the absorption of expelled or otherwise fleeing persons by other nation-states and thereby restores this universalism of inclusion.

13   The only and rare exception of this separation of the two rooms holds for the case of accepted refugees who have entered through the side door, but even so should be granted access to permanent residence permits.

14   Sometimes, however, it seems that it only takes time until economic ideas have an effect on the economy and society. Schelling (1997: 146) states that it took twenty years until economic proposals entered environmental policy. The main argument against tradable air pollution rights as market-based instruments for this policy field was the presumed immorality of making air pollution part of the market mechanism and 'to make money out of pollution'.

15   Pareto efficiency describes the situation in which no individual can be made better off without another being made worse off. Because the described market-based system would improve the situation of most actors without making anybody worse off (except the smugglers, who deserve being made worse off) the introduction of an entrance fee system can be understood as Pareto improvement.

References

Becker, Gary (1992), 'Eintrittspreise für Immigranten. Plädoyer für einen moderaten Liberalismus', in *Der Einwanderungspolitik*, in *Neue Züricher Zeitung*, 41-42. 21.10/1.11.

Becker, Gary & Guity Nashat Becker (1996), *The Economics of Life: From Baseball to Affirmative Action to Immigration, How Real-World Issues Affect Our Everyday Lives*. McGraw-Hill Education.

Bilger, Veronika, Martin Hofmann & Michael Jandl (2005), 'Human Smuggling as a Transnational Service Industry', forthcoming in *International Migration*, Special Edition on Human Smuggling.

Bommes, Michael (2006), 'Illegale Migration in der modernen Gesellschaft — Resultat und Problem der Migrationspolitik europäischer Nationalstaaten', in Jörg Alt & Michael Bommes (Hrsg.), *Illegalität: Grenzen und Möglichkeiten der Migrationspolitik*, 95-116. Wiesbaden: VS Verlag.

Bommes, Michael (1999), 'Migration und nationaler Wohlfahrtsstaat', Ein differenzierungstheoretischer Entwurf. Wiesbaden: Westdeutscher Verlag.

Borjas, George J. (1999), 'The Economic Analysis of Immigration', in Orley Ashenfelter & David Card (Eds.), *Handbook of Labor Economics*, 1679-1769. Amsterdam: Elsevier 3.

Doomernik, Jeroen (2006), 'Open borders, close monitoring', Paper presented at the Innovative Concepts for Alternative Migration Policies Workshop, Vienna: ICMPD, 24-25 March 2006.

Downs, Anthony (1957), *An Economic Theory of Democracy*. New York: Harper & Row.

Freeman, Gary P. (1995), 'Modes of Immigration Politics in Liberal Democratic States', *International Migration Review* 29 (4): 881-902.

Frey, Bruno S. (1990), 'Ökonomie ist Sozialwissenschaft', *Die Anwendung der Ökonomie auf neue Gebiete*. München: Vahlen.

Hermann, Vivian & Uwe Hunger (2003), 'Einwanderungspolitik für Hochqualifizierte in den USA', *IMIS-Beiträge* 22: 81-98.

Hillman, Arye L. (1994), 'The Political Economy of Migration Policy', in Horst Siebert (Ed.), *A Challenge for Europe*, 263-282. Tübingen: J.C.B. Mohr Paul Siebeck.

Niskanen, William A., Jr. (1971), *Bureaucracy and Representative Government*. Chicago: Aldine-Atherton.

Petros, Melanie (2005), 'The Costs of Human Smuggling and Trafficking', *Global Migration Perspectives* 31 (April).

Pies, Ingo (1998), 'Theoretische Grundlagen demokratischer Wirtschafts- und Gesellschaftspolitik – der Beitrag Gary Beckers', in Ingo Pies & Martin Leschke (Hrsg.), *Gary Beckers ökonomischer Imperialismus*, 1-29. Tübingen: Mohr.

Pies, Ingo (1995), 'Kommentar zu Manfred Tietzel: Zur politischen Ökonomie der internationalen Migration', *Jahrbuch für Neue Politische Ökonomie*. Bd. 14: 151-153.

Rumbaut, Rubén G. (1999), 'Immigration Research in the United States: Social Origins and Future Orientations', *American Behavioral Scientist* 42(9): 1285-1301.

Schelling, Thomas (1997), 'Why Does Economics Only Help With Easy Problems?', in Peter A.G. van Bergeijk, A. Lans Bovenberg, Eric E.C. van Damme & Jarig van Sinderen (Eds.), *Economic Science and Practice: The Role of Academic Economists and Policymakers*, 134-148. Cheltenham: Edward Elgar.

Sjastaad, Larry (1962), 'The Costs and Returns of Human Migration', *The Journal of Political Economy* 70: 80-93.

Stichweh, Rudolf (1998), 'Migration, nationale Wohlfahrtsstaaten und die Entstehung der Weltgesellschaft', in Michael Bommes & Jost Halfmann (Eds.), *Migration in nationalen Wohlfahrtsstaaten. Theoretische und vergleichende Untersuchungen*, 49-61. Osnabrück: Rasch.

Stiglitz, Joseph (1998), 'Distinguished Lecture on Economics in Government: The Private Uses of Public Interests: Incentives and Institutions', *Journal of Economic Perspectives* 12 (2): 3-22.

Straubhaar, Thomas (2000), 'New Migration Needs a NEMP (A New European Migration Policy)', HWWA Discussion Paper 95.

Straubhaar, Thomas (2002), *Migration im 21. Jahrhundert*. Tübingen: Mohr Siebeck.

Straubhaar, Thomas (2003), 'Wird die Staatsangehörigkeit zu einer Klubmitgliedschaft?', in Dietrich Thränhardt & Uwe Hunger (Hrsg.), *Migration im Spannungsfeld von Globalisierung und Nationalstaat* 76-89. Wiesbaden: VS Verlag.

Conclusion

Michael Jandl[1], ICMPD

> The first step toward creating an improved future
> is developing the ability to envision it.
> (Author Uknown)

When envisioning innovative approaches to the management of migration in the 21st century, it is good to know how migration has worked in the 20th century, how it works at the beginning of the new century and how it does not. In addition, when designing new policies it is helpful to have in-depth knowledge about the current policy environment in place and to bring an understanding of the complex interplay between migration policies and migration outcomes with you. Thus, a group of migration researchers as experienced and diverse as the authors of this book is probably well-placed to master this challenge. Social scientists of various stripes and disciplines, the authors of this volume display an impressive range of credentials and knowledge on migration and migration policy that should, one could assume, guarantee successful policy innovation almost by itself.

And yet, scientific excellence, even brilliance, is by itself no guarantee for drawing up improved policy proposals. This is evident from the large number of eminent scholars, in various social science disciplines, who have never even written a line on policy innovations. In fact, from standard textbooks to the most advanced analytical toolboxes of social scientists, there are no standard recipes on how to cook up a scientific policy innovation. Innovation thus remains detached from standard scientific routines and the methods of how to envision innovative policy proposals levitate somewhere between intuitive imagination, deductive skills, prognosis and artwork. Much more than a migration researcher, however transdisciplinary he or she may be, it thus takes someone willing to go beyond his or her own research craft and to trespass into the field of policymaking.

The contributors to this volume are such trespassers. And they deserve praise for it. They are willing to put forward their ideas and imagination to public scrutiny and, sometimes, to the slaughterhouse of scathing critique. It is easier to deconstruct and criticise a daring proposal than to look for its inherent merits, and many, I suspect, will not be able to resist that temptation. Yet, in our search for innovative concepts for alternative migration policies, it is the hard path that we have to follow, if the strength of ideas is to have any impact on policy.

Besides the inherent value of each single contribution to this book, the collection of policy proposals compiled in this volume brings another significant benefit to those interested in the design of new policies. Comparing ten independently conceived migration policy proposals with each other allows us to identify those areas where they converge and agree, even if the proposed innovation may look substantially different in the end. Thus, on a meta-level, new principles for the design of innovative migration policies can be identified that combine the strengths of individual proposals, while avoiding their pitfalls. It is to these common principles that this concluding chapter is devoted.

Common themes and principles in the search for innovative migration policies

One quite obvious theme that runs through all the presentations and proposals discussed at the workshop is a general *dissatisfaction* with the current situation in migration policy. And while participants agreed that not all problems conventionally labelled as 'migration problems' can be tackled by migration policy alone – indeed many of the proposed schemes explicitly point to the complex interplay between migration and wider policy areas such as trade, welfare, labour market and development policies – all presenters were *actively looking for change*, innovative concepts and policy instruments of how to bring that change about.

For most participants, this desire for change is grounded in a sober look at reality. Indeed the second major theme that can be identified in the search for innovative migration policies is the demand for an unflattering recognition of the reality of current migration policy – the fact that migration policies fall far short of their ambitions while producing a whole range of undesired and unintended consequences. On the other hand, even when producing visions that go far beyond the imagination of current policy discourse, presenters made no claim of devising the ultimate solution for all migration policy problems (reducing irregular migration, upholding protection, accommodating public fears, etc.). What is searched for are migration policies that are better suited to reality than current policies.

A third theme that runs through all proposals is a strong refocusing on the migrant, his or her motives and the *incentive structure* that the migrant is presented with. Putting the migrant and the range of possible options a (potential) migrant can choose from at the centre of all policymaking recognises the *agency of the migrant* and is seen as a necessary prerequisite for the design of policy instruments that are not frustrated by the diverging interests – and consequently unintended behaviour – of their target group. In addition, several presenters explicitly incorporate *a life-time perspective* on migration into their proposals (temporary migration, savings goals, education, return migration, family formation, childcare, etc.). Using an *incentive-aligned approach* (whether for migration, work or remittances) will not prevent all unintended side effects of migration policy from occurring, but it is seen as a powerful instrument for reaching desired migration outcomes.

Seeing the migrant as a rational agent who responds to powerful incentives also leads to a fourth common theme in many proposals which is a *re-evaluation of the role of the nation-state* in migration policy-making and a *re-appreciation of the role of markets*. In several proposals market forces and, in particular, labour markets, play a larger role in the regulation of migration than they do currently, whereas governments are relegated to a lesser role. This seems to be perfectly in tune with the mood of the time, as governments everywhere are seen to be retreating from the provision of public goods (health care, education, transport facilities, etc.), forging new public-private partnerships and limiting their role to oversight and monitoring tasks. While in EU-internal migration (applying the concept of free movement for all Union citizens), the supremacy of market forces has long been recognised, participants recognised that it would be more difficult to extend the same principle beyond the EU. At the same time, attention is shifted from the level of the nation-state upward, to the multi-national, or downward, to the local levels.

Whatever the proposed institutional arrangement may be, a fifth common theme in many proposals is the search for the most suitable levers that policy instruments can apply for exerting real influence. Such levers are searched for either strictly within migration regimes (e.g. return investment premium, in-country processing arrangements, secure residency rights, etc.) or in other policy areas (welfare schemes, labour markets, development aid, etc.). Setting the right incentives in each of these policy areas can provide powerful leverage for the attainment of important migration policy goals, provided they are coherent and do not contradict each other.

This last point leads us to a sixth common theme in the discussion of proposed policy innovations. This is the recognition of a whole *range of migration policy goals* that an innovative policy should ideally achieve. These could be provisionally sketched as 1) labour market, integration and welfare goals in receiving countries; 2) development impact on sending countries; 3) human rights and refugee protection; 4) the reduction of irregular migration and human smuggling; and 5) public opinion and the promotion of an informed and rational public discussion. Most proposals are aimed at fulfilling – at least parts of – these goals simultaneously. In other words, they strive for an *integration of target areas* – countries of origin, countries of destination and the fluid world of migrants themselves – for which possible migration solutions are sought (colloquially also known as 'win-win-win solutions').

However, it was also recognised that there are often *trade-offs* between these goals. For example, while encouraging circular migration – through schemes such as redesigned temporary migration programmes or the free movement of labour – is often said to bring benefits to both the receiving and sending countries, as well as to the migrants, such a policy may have negative impacts on integration and the family life of migrants. Moreover, temporary migration programmes may run into difficulties when incentive structures change, when family ties are newly established or when migrants later change their minds and fail to return, thereby running counter to the attainment of the above-mentioned policy goals 1, 2 and 5. Thus, even innovative policies will not be able to fully solve some of the major dilemmas of current migration regimes, but they may help to reduce the escalating costs of migration control and avoid some of the paradoxical consequences of current regulations.

Related, though not quite the same, is a seventh theme that ran through many proposals for policy innovations. This is the need for a broad consensus on the goals and instruments of migration policy if it is to attain a sustainable outcome that is not annulled by counteracting forces. This search for consensus does not deny the existence of serious conflicts of interest among the stakeholders – which at times can even reach the level of violent conflict – but represents an attempt at constructively dealing with such conflicts in alternative ways. One proposal explicitly suggests applying principles of sustainable conflict resolution strategies in migration decision-making, while in other papers the need for multi-party consensus is recognised implicitly by reference to the prevailing public opinion or the requirement for policy instruments gaining acceptance among migrants.

This leads us to an eighth and final common theme of proposed policy innovations. None of the proposed policy options was targeted at halting or significantly reducing immigration to Europe, a goal that was unanimously seen as both undesirable and unrealistic. On the other hand, none of the proposals advocated a complete dismantling of migration controls either – not even the proposal on 'Open borders, close monitoring'. Rather, what the proposals suggest in their various forms are *new 'policy mixes'* of policy instruments and control tools. Generally, the proposed shifts *are away from border controls* and physical exclusion (as these are seen to be increasingly untenable and counterproductive), and towards new forms of regulating, tracking and monitoring the activities of migrant populations. And here is another dilemma: liberalising access to labour markets and expanding temporary work programmes will likely require closer control at the workplace; pricing entrance fees or selling visas necessitates higher document security; providing return incentives involves tackling corruption; opening up borders implies stricter internal controls, and so on. The upshot is that the new policy instruments will bring both desired and undesired consequences with them. In policy innovations, as in so much else, it is a question of finding a better balance than the current system provides.

Outlook

The existence of this book is a great testimony to the creative vision of its authors in conceptualising innovative approaches to migration policy. And the very fact that you are reading it at this very moment is a testimony to the acute demand for new visions and innovative approaches in migration policymaking.

Designed as a pioneering exercise for the development of much-needed innovative concepts for migration policymaking, the first ICMPD/IMISCOE workshop on Innovative Concepts for Alternative Migration Policies has yielded an enormous crop of innovative and potentially fruitful new ideas, which have been compiled in this book for a wide readership. It is hoped that through wide dissemination and discussion of the ideas and concepts developed before, during and after this workshop, our efforts will stimulate further debate and new thinking at the academic and the policy levels, contributing to the development of better, less contested and more successful migration policies than those currently in place.

Notes

1   Michael Jandl is Senior Research Officer at the International Centre for Migration
    Policy Development (ICMPD). The views expressed in this article are those of the
    author and participants in the workshop only, and not those of ICMPD as a Vienna-
    based intergovernmental organisation or of its member states.

Workshop programme

International Workshop on Innovative Concepts for Alternative Migration Policies

Vienna, 24./25. March 2006
IMISCOE workshop organised by: International Centre for Migration Policy Development (ICMPD), Vienna

Venue: ICMPD, Meeting Room
Gonzagagasse 1, A-1010 Vienna

Agenda

Friday, 24.3.2006
13:00-13:15   Michael Jandl: Welcome

13:15-15:15   Jeff Crisp (GCIM/UNHCR): Temporary Migration Programmes: Potential and Problems
T.J.P. van Os van den Abeelen (ACVZ, Netherlands): A New European Employment Migration Policy
Theo Veenkamp (DEMOS, UK): Managing regular and irregular migration with the People Flow approach
Discussants: A, B, C

15:15-15:30   Tea/coffee break

15:30-17:30   Franck Düvell (COMPAS Oxford, UK): Applying Sustainable Conflict Resolution Strategies in Disputes over Migration
Jonathan Chaloff (CeSPI, Italy): Co-development – a myth or a workable policy approach?
Discussants: D, E, F

19:00   Dinner

Saturday, 25.3.2006

9:30-10:00	Morning Coffee

10:00-12:00   Judith Kumin (UNHCR, Brussels): In-country "refugee" processing arrangements: a humanitarian alternative?
John Davies (MRC Sussex, UK): Listening to Southern Migrants
Rainer Münz (EB, Austria): New approaches towards migrant remittances
Discussants: G, H, I

12:00-13:30   Lunch

13:30-15:30   Jeroen Doomernik (IMES, Netherlands): Open Borders, Close Monitoring
Michael Jandl (ICMPD, Vienna): The Development Visa Scheme Revisited
Holger Kolb (IMIS, Germany): Pricing Entrance Fees for Migrants
Discussants: J, K, L

15:30-16:00   Tea/coffee break

16:00-17:00   Summary, Discussion and Outlook

18:30   Guided Tour through the city: Ian Banerjee

20:00   Dinner

Discussants
A, B, C: Eva Kamaras (MoI, Hungary)
D, E, F: Han Entzinger (European Univ., NL)
G, H, I: Jordi Garcia Martinez (EC, DG JLS)
J, K, L: Christian Schmalzl (MoI, Austria)

Conference report

Rapporteurs: Haleh Chahrokh, Radoslaw Stryjewski
and Brigitte Suter, ICMPD[1]

ICMPD/IMISCOE Workshop on Innovative Concepts for Alternative Migration Policies

Vienna, 24 and 25 March 2006

The ICMPD/IMISCOE Workshop on Innovative Concepts for Alternative Migration Policies was organised by the International Centre for Migration Policy Development (ICMPD) and held in Vienna on 24 and 25 March 2006. The workshop aimed at finding determinants of the current migratory situation and policies and, based on this knowledge, innovative ideas for a number of migration topics were presented and discussed. Presenters comprising well-known scholars of migration theory and practice, representatives of UNHCR, the European Commission and several ICMPD member states (Austria, Bulgaria, Hungary, Poland, Slovakia and Switzerland) gathered for the two-day workshop, and analysed eleven concepts dealing with new perspectives for migration management systems in Europe.

The overwhelming majority of presentations concerned labour migration, identified as the most important migration phenomenon of the last decades. Apart from complex policy projects (Veenkamp, Crisp, Van Os van den Abeelen, Doomernik), some new, specifically targeted concepts were presented. One proposal considered the migration of elderly adults (Davies); two approaches addressed entrance policy (Kolb, Jandl); while one proposal sought to introduce conflict resolution strategies (Düvell) in order to better manage crises stemming from migration phenomena. This large panorama was completed by some new perspectives on the processing of international protection cases (Kumin); opportunities for co-development policies (Chaloff); and the impact of remittances on migration trends, reasons and effects (Münz). In what follows, the eleven presentations given at the workshop are reviewed.

Jeff Crisp: 'Temporary Migration Programmes: Potential and Problems'

Temporary migration programmes (TMPs) gained a negative reputation in the years after the Second World War. This was largely due to the unintended results that the programmes had in both Germany and the US. Most of the criticism was directed at the fact that many of the temporary migrants eventually stayed in the destination country.

However, since 2000, there has again been a growing interest in TMPs in several industrialised countries, as well as the European Commission and the Global Commission on International Migration. This correlates with the interest of several labour-exporting countries, such as Bangladesh, Sri Lanka or the Philippines. Proponents state that the TMPs have the potential to create a 'win-win-win' outcome. Industrialised states, which at the moment are facing a growing demographic deficit in the labour market, would be able to fill the gaps on the labour market without having to deal with the long-term presence, the integration and also the ageing of the foreign workers. Developing countries, in turn, would be able to reduce unemployment and underemployment on their labour market, could benefit from remittances that migrants send home and, upon return, from the new skills the migrants have gained. Migrants themselves have the possibility to increase their income, gain new qualifications and broaden their experience.

Proponents are convinced that the development of global communication and transport technology of the past 40 years would favour the notion of circular migration, rather than permanent migration.

However, opponents remain sceptical and fear that TMPs would – as in the past – lead to permanent residence and family reunion. The only way to implement TMPs, they argue, is to make use of draconian measures to prevent migrants from staying in the country (such as the Gulf States). Migrant activists claim that TMPs would ultimately produce second-class citizens and would favour limited migrant rights and social exclusion. Furthermore, labour market implications for natives are considered, and it is argued, in addition, that irregular migration will be accelerated as regular migration might boost irregular migration through the creation of networks. Also, there is no clear proof of the beneficial effects of remittances on development. Moreover, the social splitting of families due to migration is a social cost that cannot be neglected either.

Crisp therefore presents the prerequisites for a better functioning TMP. In his view, TMPs should not be left to market forces alone; he rather sees state involvement in the labour market as a prerequisite. Further, potential migrants should be clearly informed about their rights, the conditions, and the obligation to return. As Crisp points out, successful future TMPs should provide for an equal treatment of migrants, e.g. same salary, same working conditions including medical benefits, etc. Inspections and employers' sanctions should be implemented to guarantee this. Also, there should be a protection of jobs for EU nationals. The length of these contracts has to be considered carefully: it should be a restricted length that covers all costs that the migrants had, but should not be long enough for the migrant to integrate into the new society. Migrants should also have the chance to change employers through transferable work permits, rather than binding them to one employer and fostering dependency on employers. Furthermore, portable pensions and saving systems and a new visa regime that allows migrants to circulate between the country of destination and the home country are further measures to seduce temporary migrants to go back. Finally, the asylum channel should still be open, and people should be able to change their type of residence permit (e.g. become a student, marry a national, etc.).

Workshop participants pointed out that the main reason why the guestworker system in Germany resulted in many migrants staying was the imposed restrictions on movement at the end of the programme. This caused a considerable number of the migrant workers to stay in the country of destination.[2] Therefore, a new TMP with emphasis on circular migration is highly welcomed. An important question with regard to Crisp's TMP is how flexible the system will be in terms of changing the purpose of residence (from worker to student to spouse). Regarding the length, it was argued that it very much depends on the migrant's personal circumstances; in some cases, already a stay of three months could make sense. However, at this point it was argued that this could be a problem for employers, as trainings are cost-intensive, and employers are therefore interested in retaining workers as long as possible.[3]

If the EU is to implement such a programme, concrete concepts are needed to clarify 'who are the people that we want to integrate, and who are the people that we would like to see in a TMP'. Also, with an EU-wide TMP, increased partnership is needed. The scenario was painted of the UK taking over a substantial number of skilled labour from one of the new EU Member States, which might leave the latter in need of temporary workers from abroad. In that case, it has to be clear for the UK to co-operate in an EU-wide TMP.

T.J.P. van Os van den Abeelen: 'A New European Employment Migration Policy'

T.J.P. van Os van den Abeelen considers the economic discrepancies between regions as the main reason for contemporary migration flows. The current migration control systems promoted by the prosperous states are not efficient, and they cannot be so in view of the general will of many in less prosperous parts of world to escape poverty and uncertain futures. A paradoxical effect of control measures in immigration countries is an increase of abuse of the asylum systems as well as a growth of irregular entrances and irregular employment. The methods of entrance, that basically are unfounded asylum applications, forced or 'paper' marriages or simply irregular stay and employment, result in concrete political, social and economic problems. The current challenge for migration policy is to find a right solution in the continuum between inefficient state control as applied up to the present and the utopia of a world without borders – the main target of such a policy being the combating of illegal foreign presence and employment. Especially the Southern European countries seem to be exposed to large irregular migration flows (consecutive regularisations in Spain and Italy do not solve the problem), which implies a need to elaborate new migration approaches.

In view of the demographic decline in all European countries, migration should be generally recognised as a positive phenomenon. Currently, two trends can be observed: a strict control of the massive flows of economic immigration, on the one hand, and attempts to seduce highly skilled migrants to the EU countries, on the other hand. The public position towards migration phenomenon should be taken into consideration as well. From this perspective, not economic, but rather social and cultural problems are often arguments against immigration.

A precondition for the sustainable migration management in the future is a reduction of the economic fissures between regions of immigration and emigration, a goal to be reached only in close interlinkage between various policies: migration policies, but also policies for trade, economics, development, etc.

From the migration policy side, the solution could be a system of temporary employment migration, with stress on the return circumstances facilitating migrant economic reinsertion in the country of origin's economic system as an active actor of development.

Van den Abeelen's proposal is a residence permit valid exclusively in the issuing EU country for a period of a maximum of seven years, which will determine its immigration quota. The criteria of admission would be established as a function of the following factors: preference for nationals of countries that will benefit from migrant knowledge, experience and capital acquired in his or her immigration country, as well as for literate migrants with – if needed – some professional knowledge or experience. While on EU territory, migrants would be provided with the right to free education and professional training. The migrant's stay and work on EU territory would result in payment of an investment premium available after the migrant's actual return to his or her origin country. A rough calculation of the accumulated return premium available after seven years indicates that it would be in the order of some € 30,000. A possibility of having access to a favourable credit system in addition to the investment premium could be considered. This temporary migration system should be correlated with measures combating illegal stay and illegal employment (both illegal stay/ work and illegal employment should be penalised).

The proposed system is trying to satisfy both the needs of developed countries (flexible economic migration system in view of labour force shortages) and developing countries (a considerable assistance in addition to the conventional aid for development offered by the EU Member States), but is obviously not free of deficiencies concerning all parties: migrants can stay in receiving countries in spite of incentives to return; receiving countries can be unable to fully control migration flows and the effectiveness of investments by migrants is doubtful when countries of origin might try to use their migrants' allocations improperly.

Concerning Van den Abeelen's proposal, discussants underlined a need at the EU level for an efficient temporary labour migration system. The European Commission has already undertaken some steps in this direction by elaborating a proposed approach to migration and development. In its concept of 'migration profiles' it suggests evaluating the situation of the labour market of given third countries and bringing together relevant information on migration issues with special attention to the brain drain phenomenon. The discussants opted for a stronger involvement of the source countries in the reintegration process, providing returning migrants with more possibilities, financial support facilitating an easier start, tax benefits, etc. From this perspective, the future cooperation between immigration and emigration countries is seen as a partnership rather than one-way flows of finances, social and educational capital.

One of the doubts raised concerned the public attitude towards such a proposal. Potential migrants, being young and starting their jobs, would need substantial amounts for their professional training – areas in which countries might also lack resources for their own citizens. Yet, the idea that they would not be seriously rooted (founding families, engaging in financial obligations such as loans or mortgages) during the seven-year stay in Europe was considered to be unrealistic. Moreover, the proposed duration for maximum length of stay for labour migrants (seven years) was considered too long when compared to the relevant EU directive that grants a special status to third-country nationals after five years. It was suggested that the length of stay with a TMP be between the short period of seasonal work and the long-term residence category.

Van den Abeelen argued that, in the present situation of emigration countries, investment is needed and money for consumption provided by emigrants' remittances is not enough for assuring a durable development. The investments should be productive and, in the long-term, create more employment opportunities, which would consequently attract potential migrants to return home.

An important remark concerned the possibility of failure of the returned migrant's investment. In such a case people would obviously try to come back to the immigration country, rendering the proposal inefficient with regard to the illegal stay reduction. One of the answers to this obstacle could be more training on how to invest.

Another question highlighted the structural discrepancies in countries of origin, which contravene the stated co-development principles (that development should be sustainable and benefit all).

Critical remarks concerned also the practical value of this proposal. As a fact, Europe needs mainly (intermediate and highly) skilled migrants. These people, however, can normally stay and are therefore not a problem for return. In this light, a question was raised regarding what Van den Abeelen's proposal actually changes. In response, Van den Abeelen argued that skilled migrants are not included in this project. The proposal, nevertheless, offers a solution to many social and economic problems: migrants, for instance, do not age in the receiving country, which means fewer costs for social security, and the money they get upon return contributes to the development of their home country.

Theo Veenkamp: 'Managing regular and irregular migration with the People Flow approach'

Theo Veenkamp's presentation took up the same topic as Van den Abeelen's proposal but with different thinking. The concept presented in the workshop is a revised version of the first 'People Flow Report' of 2003. It is based on two starting points: the complex nature of modern migration flows and the inefficient migration management carried out by nation-states. The characteristics of contemporary migration movements are: steady increase of migration scale and scope, new forms (more temporary and circular migration than permanent) and increasing numbers of irregular migrants who, however, are able to arrange for their lives within the receiving countries' economic and social systems. The latter gives evidence of the failure of current migration policies. In addition, the stagnant definitions of voluntary and forced migration should be reformulated.

The present migration management should be understood as a system in which disproportional emphasis is put on control measures, which Veenkamp calls a 'dangerous illusion'. The outdated concept of a homogenous nation-state with a single culture painfully gives way to the factual diversity and transnationalism. Another big issue and big failure of the migration strategies implemented up to the present is the migrants' integration. The question of how to assure all the elements indispensable for successful integration remains open.

In view of the above mentioned, the People Flow strategy tries to offer a new approach. The major need identified by Veenkamp is to create a situation of mutual benefit for migrants, the country of origin as well as the receiving country, achieved through the efficient capitalisation of human resources and cultural diversity and the reasonable use of migrants' input into their economies of origin. The core question of the People Flow approach is the understanding of the migrants' motivations and mechanisms of receiving/arriving population interaction. The postulated innovation is to change governments' management strategies from border control to migration flow control and open the migration management system by introducing non-governmental partners. The improving possibilities to do so offered by new technologies have been underlined.

The innovative People Flow approach suggests restructuring the present thinking on migrants' admission into two tracks: one for target-oriented migrants and another one for so-called 'explorers' (an unorthodox denomination for the innovatively perceived irregular migrants). The first track addresses those migrants that have a clear motivation to migrate. For this track, a decisive privatisation of admission management is recommended. The second track, meant for the potential irregular migrants, addresses those who have neither a predetermined goal nor a clear counterpart apart from their private (family, friends) migration networks. The innovation of the concept relies on providing 'explorers' with a new category of legal status striking a balance between the inconveniences of the orthodox irregular stay and current residents' fears about competition by explorers in the labour market. Such an 'explorer' status should provide: registration at a private agency specialised in 'explorer' issues (registration, realistic information on possibilities, assistance); a modest net salary; a gross salary, equal for all employees doing the same work; help with remittance transfer. The status would not provide social security nor a pension scheme. The migrant would not be integrated into the taxation system either. In order to level the disproportion in explorers' and conventional residents' access to the social system, the following solution is foreseen: the difference between net and gross salaries could be managed by the migrants' agency and transferred into basic health care, basic education, etc.

In Veenkamp's presentation, discussants identified as a real advantage the suggested necessity to understand migrants' reasons, needs and expectations, concepts rarely discussed at a governmental level. It has been underlined that receiving countries have some responsibilities; when accepting people, they should be aware of cultural implications – the recent Prophet's caricatures crisis should be mentioned as a very serious cross-cultural misunderstanding. While trying to find possible obstacles for a successful implementation of the People Flow approach, discussants emphasised that the different levels of migration policymaking (which is not only the responsibility of national governments) depend, to a certain extent, on the future voters' points of view. This is especially crucial to note in light of the current discourse of fear caused by the 'stranger' intrusion into national communities, strengthened by present security problems and social troubles of the welfare states. Voters should be provided with the following information: who are the migrants, what do they want (opportunities they want to exploit in the receiving country), what can they offer thereto (filling up labour market shortages, etc.)? The strong interlinkage between anti-migration attitudes and media coverage was highlighted in this context. The discussants agreed that high-level consultations are needed but that national administrations lean on officers who should understand this background. As a consequence, appropriate distribution of information (possibly including trainings) for journalists and other opinion leaders would be needed.

The suggested privatisation of the migration management was a source of some discussants' doubts. Recourse to the PPP concept (private-public partnership) as opposed to the suggested involvement of private agencies was evoked as a possible solution.

The system of People Flow, theoretically very attractive, has also been perceived as difficult to be implemented due to the economic differences between immigration and emigration regions. It could perfectly work between Europe and the US where the discrepancies in life standards are less accentuated. The discussants also wondered about the real efficiency of the People Flow approach with regard to the reduction of irregular migration. The risk of excessive bureaucracy discouraging migrants to get registered was pointed out, along with the People Flow strategy's impact on the refugee system.

Veenkamp stated that if the People Flow strategy were to be implemented, the number of asylum applications would decrease significantly. Regarding irregular migration it was underlined that it obviously will exist, and it is the innovative system's challenge to seduce migrants into registration. As the People Flow strategy is a 'no control' approach, the bureaucracy should not be a discouraging factor. As foreseen, this system should create fewer problems for politicians than the operational problems now. Its open and reliable methods should convince the voting population that they see what happens and what will happen – an essential factor for the elections – which should neutralise voters' fears.

Franck Düvell: 'Applying Sustainable Conflict Resolution Strategies in Disputes over Migration'

Franck Düvell's presentation criticised more recent approaches of conventional migration policies focusing on migration management, especially the structural exclusion of migrants from decision-making processes. Moreover, he rejected interpretations of the principle of 'freedom of movement' for its radical individualism missing political regulation and control. Instead, analysing migration as a social conflict, he suggested a method that aims to address the conflict by way of sustainable conflict resolution strategies, which are characterised by integrating all stakeholders, in particular migrants, into the decision-making process and which are based upon consensus processes for the mutual benefits of all.

Recent events (at the borders of the Spanish exclaves Ceuta and Melilla or similar events at the Greek-Albanian border, the US-Mexican border, German-Polish border, etc.) show clearly the conflict potential in migration, whereas present migration control appears inefficient, expensive and ethically problematic.

In this respect, two approaches are generally suggested: managed migration and freedom of movement – i.e. liberalising (economic) migration. There have been several initiatives in the last few years on suggested managed migration models, but most have the characteristic in common that migrants are excluded from policy designing and making. Managed migration is strict regimes, while irregular migration is ongoing, resulting in conflicting aims and no real solution. The other presented alternatives are, as mentioned before, freedom of movement, hence liberalisation of migration. Düvell criticises that few of these models indicate how this could work in praxis. Persons who migrate often try to escape from misery, but then also often end up in misery, without a solution. Freedom of movement in this context represents individualism, and migrants are put into unregulated competition – with winners and losers.

Based on these arguments, Düvell suggests enlisting sustainable conflict resolution strategies as an alternative. One has to introduce a concept to reconcile and reach a consensus, based on a high level of compromise, communication and participation of all stakeholders. Indeed, the outcome has to be mutually acceptable, while acknowledging (not eliminating) the differences. Some principles of sustainable conflict resolution strategies are e.g. based on voluntary participation, offering equal opportunities as well as tolerance and respect for diverse interests, etc. The method most commonly used in conflict resolution is the round table of all significant stakeholders. The round table setting should tackle unequal power relations, which shall thereby be neutralised. Düvell applies this also to issues of migration.

Such a dialogue is presented as an adequate method to address conflicts over migration issues in various settings, e.g. when people feel the need to migrate but before they make a choice where to go and before they leave; when migrants turn up at the border; when migrants have already crossed an international border; or when migrants wish or are expected to return. Anybody who is involved and affected by migration processes has to be included and addressed by the dialogue. It is not acceptable to exclude migrants or any stakeholders on legal arguments or financial grounds. It should be a flexible process. Time and space must be allocated to each stakeholder to consult with their constituency and to voice their concerns to the other side – countries of destination and sending countries, and all this also on public TV. The actual challenge lies in the diverse interests and perspectives of governments, migrants, businesses, etc. At the end of a sustainable conflict resolution process, agreeable solutions should be found (not focusing on holistic solutions).

Finally, one should also consider the creation of new institutions, which are not associated with any of the conflicting parties. That could also mean, for example, reforming or providing with an extended mandate an existing institution, such as the UN. However, it is not necessary to engage the round table at a global level, but one should take into account the regionalisation of migration processes – not countries but regions are linked through migration – in these conflict resolution processes.

Düvell additionally pointed out that quite a number of examples exist where sustainable conflict resolution round tables are already applied: e.g. round table meetings in Portugal or at the local level in Lausanne and Fribourg (Switzerland) and France (including illegal migrants).

In brief, sustainable conflict resolution is about seeing a conflict from the other party's perspective. With respect to immigration, the goal is to try to develop outcomes that enable populations to coexist. The aim is to find a solution in which no one loses, in which no one is worse off and in which ideally everyone gains something.

The main discussant sketched the presented approach in a first reaction as unrealistic, or daring. Favourably noted was the fact that sustainability is addressed, since this is normally often overlooked. Five main criticisms have been made: firstly, which definition of conflict is used? Is it really solely a clash of interests? Is this not always the case with human interactions and, if so, it cannot always be solved. Secondly, freedom of movement is not advocated. This, in turn, means that there has to be selectivity, which has the implication that there will always be those who are allowed to enter and those who are not. Thirdly, even when all the stakeholders get around the table and discuss, Düvell's proposal will hardly work: there will always be more and less powerful stakeholders. And those who are more powerful are not likely to give up their power. To this point, Düvell acknowledged that power relations are difficult to address, but also doubted if governments really do have power over human agency. Migrants also have power and gain power by vetoing. Fourthly, communities have the right to their own future. At which stage shall we allow these new persons to discuss the future of the society? Certainly not from the first day, but there has to be a time when this is possible. Fifthly, bilateral agreements and the local level were stressed. The city of Rotterdam was put forward as an interesting example in this regard: it is the only city in the Netherlands with a considerable number of Cape Verdians, which would favour direct business relations between the city of Rotterdam and Cape Verde. Düvell acknowledges that cities are definitely in different situations than central governments. Cities in the north or south of Germany, for instance, are in very different situations concerning the wish for more or less migration.

Another discussant pointed out that the current discussion goes more towards limiting the number of international organisations. In this regard, it could make more sense to make use of already existing ones. Düvell's argument for a new institution stresses that the negative image, which currently existing institutions have with some of the stakeholders, makes it impossible for them to chair the round table.

One discussant described Düvell's approach as applied philosophical policy and expressed interest in further information on respective examples at the local level. Düvell pointed out that there are examples in France in this regard of a social dialogue with all stakeholders, from top down, talking to each other, not only border guards and migrants. For facilitating conflict resolution, all have to have a say.

Finally, Düvell emphasises that further research would be needed to be able to provide more detailed examples in this respect – especially regarding the cases of Fribourg, Lausanne, France and Portugal – which he would be willing and interested to undertake.

Jonathan Chaloff: 'Co-development – a myth or a workable policy approach?'

Jonathan Chaloff's presentation provided an outline of recent thinking on the co-development concept and principles, as well as some actual examples of new policy approaches. His paper is the result of work on concrete projects and a search for the positive impact of existing policies.

The term 'co-development' was used first by the French in the 1980s, and the policy was initially directed primarily towards diminishing the 'root causes' of migration. In the meanwhile, the policy concept has developed, aiming at migration's positive impact on sending countries and countries of destination. How can both countries develop and benefit?

Chaloff first addressed the question of who decides the length of stay of migrants. Every migrant has a different time-line and target (before returning). And indeed circular migration is seen as positive for co-development. However, this is difficult to discuss in the current political framework. Receiving countries and their laws and policies rarely take into account the plans of the migrants. Sending countries do not consider this either. In negotiations, their primary interest focuses only on the access of their nationals to the respective country. Therefore, one has to work on both sides.

Procedural changes can also affect mobility and migration: visa delays for instance can discourage returns, and the wish of some migrants to save their holidays for longer trips to their home countries is perceived negatively by some employers.

Chaloff also addressed the concept of the migrant as 'development agent', i.e. as being active for his or her home country. The problematic point of this concept is the fact that there is no control over the individual migrant regarding the facts of how much the migrant does care about the home country or how the money earned is spent. Therefore, the focus should not be on the individual, but on the entire community. Several relevant projects exist in this regard. Chaloff outlined, for instance, one project among others in Albania, where a student association arranges short internships and apprenticeships in public administration and private businesses at home for Albanian students abroad. Students are exposed to job opportunities in their home countries and institutions are exposed to their standards abroad as well as critical judgments.

Migration happens from one local community to another local community in the destination country. Local authorities, therefore, have more power and autonomy in this regard, as is, for instance, the case in Italy. There are a number of examples of low-scaled projects. In some of them the diaspora community has to come up with parts of the funding for projects in their home country.

In brief, it has to be noted that policymakers in receiving countries do not often think about issues outside of their area of concern and national interest. Similarly, sending countries might be more interested in sending population out of the country, than dealing with return. Migrants often do not consider investment (or return) because of weak institutions in home countries as well as human rights issues and corruption. Stakeholders on round tables can play a role, but then the question is raised who represents these circular migrants, which is one of the reasons why they were ignored so far. People active in the area of migration and in the area of development should interact even more. Finally, policy approaches should emphasise possible positive co-development effects on sending and destination countries.

The main discussant stressed that in this migration policy debate it becomes obvious that the concept of the nation-state is not really adequate to deal with it, but that there is no substitute for it. Local actors do play a role, whereas nation-states are less relevant for migration policies but more for integration and social policies. There are a number of studies that make clear that migrants are trapped in the EU countries because they would lose security and income if they returned. Circular migrants present a specific structure, similar to issues of dual citizenship (exclusive/multiple loyalties).

Another discussant raised the question about the reason behind the booming migration and development debate: is it the large amount of remittances which was noticed only in recent years or the aim to give up conventional approaches? Is it a sustainable debate?

Moreover, circular migrant organisations do exist already, and they could be the representations mentioned. Chaloff acknowledges that transnational organisations are stakeholders, but that one has to consider this carefully, since they often tend to represent themselves or are even 'empty' organisations.

The vision was expressed by yet another discussant to turn the alleged disadvantage of multiple loyalties into an advantage (also concerning citizenship) by considering these persons as active promoters of democracy.

Another workshop participant explained that, on the EU level, the persons working in the area of migration and development meet frequently (RELEX, AIDCO, etc.). In particular, there are programmes like AENEAS for that. One recent project under this programme in Andalusia dealt with workers for strawberry fields from Morocco and facilitated cooperation and mechanisms to return between specific villages in Morocco and in Spain.

Another discussant addressed the question of who decides in conflicting interests in this area, and asked whether mediation is possible in reality. Finally, Chaloff mentioned transnational welfare as an interesting topic for further research.

Rainer Münz: 'New approaches towards migrant remittances'

In his presentation, Rainer Münz also touched upon the issue of migration and development, concentrating however on financial flows.

There are 190 million migrants spread around the world. An estimated 500 to 600 million people depend on remittances sent by their relatives working abroad. From the total of 231 billion dollars sent as remittances in 2004, 171 billion, i.e. 80 per cent, reached low-income countries. The remittances phenomenon is steadily growing with annual growth rates of 8 to 9 per cent while the other financial sources coming from high-income countries (FDI, ODA, investments flow) are vulnerable to fluctuations.

The above-mentioned amount of remittances cannot be more than imperfect estimations due to the different channels (more or less formal) of transferring money to the countries of origin. The main receiving countries are China, India, Mexico, Philippines and South Korea. For some countries (Tonga, Palestinian territory) the share of remittances in GDP reaches around 40 per cent. Israel, Tonga and Barbados head the list of major recipients of remittances per capita.

Positive short-term economic effects of remittances are: growing consumption, poverty reduction and currency effects (dollarisation/euroisation of local economies). Among long-term effects, indirect growth effect through consumption, positive impacts on investment (depending, however, on local economic stability) as well as less unemployment and improved legal framework should be enumerated.

As negative impacts, remittances can cause a reduction of foreign exchange reserves, accentuate income discrepancies between families with and families without members abroad, the 'Dutch disease' effect and, as already mentioned above, dollarisation/euroisation of the economy.

The current remittances flows, seen globally as a positive phenomenon, lead in consequence to the following policy conclusions: there is a need to promote legal migration (through, for instance, networks of bilateral/multilateral agreements), as well as to promote circular migration due to the empirical observation that circular migrants send home more. Other issues to be tackled are to get diasporas engaged with their historical homelands, to promote transparent and reliable systems of transfer, as well as to address the brain drain and a lack of possibilities for win-win solutions.

The discussants' remarks concerned the need for reducing transaction costs in order to encourage migrants to send remittances through formal and transparent channels. In the discussion reference was made to the Spanish government's troubles to convince immigrants to contribute to co-development funds with their transfers. Doubts were raised regarding the negative impact of remittances on local entrepreneurship when it is more comfortable to receive money from abroad. In the same line, it was underlined that, on the one hand, remittances could support local dictatorial regimes and, on the other hand, they could even increase poverty (as in the case of Armenia). A counter-argument to these doubts could be the Israeli case; equally, neither in India nor in China do remittances have negative impacts on growth or economic reforms.

In retrospective, Münz raised many of the same points made in relation to co-development. For example, when it comes to increasing remittance levels, circular migration should be promoted based on the empirical observation that circular migrants send home more. Likewise, promoting the productive use of remittances in homelands or stimulating investment by migrants in public projects is seen as problematic as the migrants sending the remittances have their own legitimate priorities for using their hard-earned money. Here, too, fostering translocal links is seen as the best way of getting diasporas engaged with their historical homelands. In a more critical perspective, remittances must be seen as having not only positive economic impacts on home countries (increased consumption, poverty reduction, etc.) but also negative impacts (increasing income disparities, de-motivation effects on local entrepreneurship, etc.) that should be dealt with.

Judith Kumin: 'In-country "refugee" processing arrangements:
a humanitarian alternative?'

In her presentation, Judith Kumin noted that measures taken by industrialised countries to prevent irregular migration do not distinguish between persons seeking protection and other categories of people on the move. The need to provide access to asylum risks being neglected in the predominantly economic- and labour-oriented discourse on migration. In the presenter's opinion, countries with highly restrictive migration policies have a moral, if not legal, obligation to soften these restrictions with humanitarian protection measures. One such measure could be the establishment of mechanisms to admit persons in need of protection directly from their countries of origin.

The resettlement of refugees from first countries of asylum has traditionally been seen as a kind of safety valve, but is increasingly controversial. Although it without doubt provides refugee protection and burden-sharing with countries of first asylum, resettlement has also become a target of criticism. Some observers see resettlement as a pull factor and as limiting the effectiveness of voluntary return programmes. Moreover, the possibility of fraud, as well as security threats in refugee camps (where not everybody can be selected), should not be neglected. In this context, Kumin asks whether the resettlement of 'refugees' directly from their country of origin might be a promising measure.

Advantages of this proposal consist of providing protection for people in need and discouraging persons in need of protection from taking the risk of the often dangerous journey in search of refuge. In regions threatened by humanitarian crises, this measure could reduce refugee pressures and inter-state tensions. Such programmes could spare refugees the hardship associated with a stay in a first country of asylum. Furthermore, the condition of a minimum level of cooperation between countries of origin and receiving countries could contribute to strengthening international relations and reinforcing respect for basic human rights.

The main objections arise from the fact that such in-country processing could serve as an alibi for even more restrictive measures by asylum countries to block asylum seekers' access to their territories. There is also the risk of attention being drawn to candidates for departure who might be at risk at the hands of authorities in countries of origin. Finally, such programmes require the cooperation of authorities in countries of origin, which might not be forthcoming.

Being aware of all these risks and inconveniences, Kumin suggests that the proposal could still be worth pursuing in the framework of European efforts to expand prospects for legal migration. The example of the UNHCR-Vietnam Memorandum of Understanding setting up the Orderly Departure Programme in 1979, as well as the US and Canadian experiences with source country processing arrangements lead Kumin to this conclusion. Whether European countries would undertake such programmes remains to be seen. The fact that traditional refugee resettlement is still underutilised in Europe – in spite of The Hague Programme's recommendation – does not bode well.

The discussants of Kumin's presentation agreed that either in South-North or East-West migration movements there are still people who meet the criteria of the 1951 Refugee Convention, thus there would be candidates for orderly departure arrangements. Some discussants took a more optimistic view of possible expanded European involvement in resettlement schemes. It was mentioned that the European Refugee Fund will be modified in this direction. Quoting the example of France, it was stated that many European countries have little or no experience with resettlement, which implies need of assistance. Others saw difficulties in reaching consensus on the countries to be targeted for orderly departure arrangements, and made a link to the EU problems with elaborating a common list of 'safe countries of origin'.

John Davies: 'Listening to Southern Migrants'

John Davies outlined a moral deficit of current migration approaches based on ambiguous human rights interpretations and insufficient attention paid to the migrants' opinions and needs, resulting in migration contests and crises. His proposal, starting from the study of Albanian elderly, draws a picture of pensioners as mere recipients of remittances sent by younger generations; victims of care drain, worthless in their roles of parents and grandparents and inactive though still of working age (in their fifties). In view of the above, Davies postulates the establishment of a more flexible migration policy towards the elderly.

In the current political discourse, migration is perceived as a problem. The need of return and non-settlement measures is seen as crucial. Another important question of debates on migration is social integration of the immigrants who are often seen as a threat for the host country security. Encouraging migration of elderly could be a response to these concerns. The family background in the receiving country could prevent young migrants from engaging in criminal activities. The stronger links with the country of origin provided by the older generation should serve as an incentive to return. The complete family would be able to better manage the income as well as to better plan the labour division between its members, bringing, as one of its consequences, higher female labour force participation in host country labour markets. Such a policy should be rendered successful by the introduction of flexible mechanisms of admission that would give migrants the impression of rules stability, which would impede the strategy of durable settlement. In Davies' approach all countries contiguous to the European Union could be beneficiaries of such a policy.

The negative sides of such an approach would be the reinforcement of existing social inequalities, young migrants' reduced interest for integration through rooting them deeper in the home country traditions as well as the danger of inappropriate skills for effective childcare.

The discussants underlined as a positive fact that the motives of migrants themselves are taken seriously. Davies' proposal tries to reduce the inter-regional and social frictions, postulated in several previous presentations. Flexibility in 'selling' EU migration policies to migrants and a need of not being perceived as an exclusively Western club that the others do not want to listen to were highlighted as well.

It was pointed out that there is an increasing number of irregular migrants above the age of 50 in Germany and elsewhere, a case that confirms Davies' hypothesis on more stable labour market strategies of elderly migrants as well their resistance towards the criminal milieu.

Once again, the public opinion was evoked, especially in the context of possible threats for social insurance and social security systems that elderly migrants could cause. In Davies' argumentation, the importance of the social security system is a myth; moreover, the unemployed young migrants can constitute a bigger danger for security systems than their professionally stable parents or grandparents.

Jeroen Doomernik: 'Open Borders, Close Monitoring'

At the moment, policies and practices of migration control are manifold in the EU Member States. There is, however, a general agreement under the current regime that restrictive policies are required in order to tackle 'the problem' of migration. The political climate is such that migration, in fact, is connected to 'problems' and 'threats to security, the economy and the labour market'.

Nevertheless, the prevailing measures have not proven to hinder migrants from coming. On the contrary, these restrictive control measures currently 'produce' more irregular migration in the Southern EU states, while they 'create' asylum seekers in the Northern EU states. Furthermore, migration has become more expensive (in terms of smuggling fees for migrants and asylum procedure costs in application countries), and more dangerous (thousands of people have died while trying to reach Europe). Moreover, Doomernik thinks that the asylum systems all over Europe have deteriorated in the past decades, thereby failing to adequately protect those in need of such protection.

This is why Doomernik makes the case for open borders. Everybody who is in the country, he says, would be legal. He applies two fundamental criteria: the moral and the practical. The moral liberal criterion states that there must be severe grounds for a justified limitation to an individual's freedom of movement or infringement of his or her liberties, be it a citizen or an alien. In practical terms, open migration can be argued for by the cost effectiveness of the proposal, in fact, Doomernik's concept requires much lower costs in the field of migration control.

From an economist's point of view, the labour market should be left alone in order to benefit all parties involved. The protection of the natives on the labour market is a very powerful and often invoked argument against open borders. However, as Doomernik points out, research has shown in both cases that imported labour tends to be complementary to native labour, and little evidence of wage-dumping was found. Therefore, Doomernik sees no justification – other than to lessen the fears invoked earlier – to restrict access of immigrants to the labour market.

However, there is one exception. In welfare states different rules apply. Since welfare states cannot afford to provide for all migrants coming through open borders, migrants should first pay insurance and taxes for a certain time (to be defined), before they themselves can benefit from the system. For a while, they would be second-class citizens, but – so Doomernik's argument goes – this is already reality: in the Netherlands around 1.5 per cent of the population has an irregular status.

Opponents of this proposal would argue that Europe would not have the capacity to host 'everybody'. However, Doomernik counters this argument by pointing out that open borders would also create more (return) emigrants.

Of course, open borders also demand some few basic rules: everybody is welcome, unless he or she poses a serious threat to society or breaches the law. In this case, the person should be expelled. It is therefore important to create a common database in which all migrants are registered with biometric data. Refugees in need of protection have the chance to apply for asylum when registering.

The discussant clarified that his concept more or less already applies to the EU as a common market and area of free movement for Union citizens. The question is now whether it is to be extended to the whole world (the so-called third countries outside the EU). One consequence of this proposal is that the border guards will be out of work. They could, however, be used in the field of the labour market, such as to implement sanctions and make inspections. In fact, as Doomernik recognises, open borders would not eliminate control measures entirely; rather they would imply a redirection of control measures from external borders to internal controls, especially on the labour market.

A problem with this proposal identified by a discussant is seen in the fact that people in a welfare state cannot be excluded from certain public goods, such as streets, security, etc. Therefore, it is suggested, it would make more sense to put a price on the use of all the collective goods.

A moral dilemma is also connected with the question of what to do with people that end up outside the system. In this case NGOs could take over some tasks. Of course, as was brought up by another participant, the question applies here: what consequences do we prefer? Yet another opponent mentioned the possible reluctance of people to register due to increased bureaucracy. Doomernik, however, suggests creating sufficient incentives to register, such as no work authorisation without registration.

Michael Jandl: 'The Development Visa Scheme Revisited'

The DV Scheme proposes a market-based migration control policy whose objective is to tackle irregular migration, to substitute irregular migration for legal migration and to cut out human smugglers.

Today the facilitation of illegal entry into states for profit by human smugglers accounts for the overwhelming share of illegal entries to European countries. Human smuggling activities – even if they do not lead to trafficking in human beings – imply the following problems: they have been linked to organised crime, they pose a threat to sovereignty and the internal security of states, and they exploit human beings in desperate situations. Human smuggling is a highly lucrative business. For example, several thousand euros are paid from Eastern European countries to reach Western Europe, and despite the high sum of money paid, the journey is often dangerous and time-consuming. Furthermore, the money paid to the smugglers constitutes a considerable drain on already scarce resources for development in the countries of origin.

The DV Scheme therefore aims to curtail irregular migration and human smuggling; a reduction of migration in general is not suggested. Rather it proposes an innovative approach for substituting irregular migration by regular, authorised migration.

The rules that Jandl puts forward are simple. Anyone who wishes to migrate should be able to buy a legal entry permit (Development Visa) at roughly the price of currently prevailing smuggling fees. The DV Scheme is not exclusive, which means *anyone* eligible can apply for it. Other 'free' visa systems (e.g. student, tourist, migrant worker) could run parallel to it. All the applicants will be fingerprinted. In that way, visa violations (overstay, etc.) can be tracked, and non-complying DV holders will be excluded from the scheme in the future. The DV is an all-purpose visa, i.e. it is not tied to the labour market. However, if the DV holder is found to engage in irregular employment, he or she will be expelled from further participation in the DV Scheme. There will be a quota system, with the quota lying at a similar magnitude as the current demand for smuggling services. Lastly, the DVs will be issued for one host country only. It will be the task of the EU JLS Council to decide on the quotas for every host country each year.

The core of the DV concept lies in the tripartion of the DV fees. The fees for the DV are to be divided into three equal parts. One-third will go to targeted development programmes in the sending country. Another third is a return incentive and will be reimbursed as a starting help to the DV holder upon return. Should the DV holder not return within the specified time limit of the DV (for reasons such as overstaying, gain of legal residence in the host country through marriage or work related stay, etc.) the money will not be reimbursed. Lastly, one-third will go to the DV Social Security Deposit (DVSSD), which will cover basic social security, such as medical costs in cases of emergency only.

If the migrant, however, takes up legal employment and pays regular social security contributions, the last third (from DVSSD) will be reimbursed upon return as well. This is, according to Jandl, a clear incentive for migrants to take up legal work.

In order to apply this scheme to reality, the issuing of DVs has to be coordinated among the EU Member States. Then, quotas for every country of origin and every country of destination have to be agreed upon, and adjusted after every year. Prices of the visas have to be settled, and time limits for stays have to be agreed upon. Jandl suggests a limited time frame between one and three years.

It is important to mention that under the DV Scheme, the asylum channel could be accommodated as well. One option could be that DV holders could apply for asylum, and if asylum status is granted, they would receive a full refund of the DV fees plus integration assistance. However, if their application is rejected, they would lose the right to stay in the host country and would not get any reimbursement from the DV Scheme apart from the return incentive.

Jandl's DV Scheme requires the full cooperation of the source countries in its implementation. Therefore, the DV Scheme should not be applied in failed states or states that systematically violate the human rights of their citizens.

The main discussant commented that the holistic view of the proposal is innovative, but since holistic approaches to migration management are quite new, there is not much experience yet. One interesting observation addressed the possible competition among sending states for the quotas (as higher visa quotas directly result in more money for development). Another question raised was whether or not to include people in transit. If they were to be included it has to be decided to which country the development sum goes.

The concept, however, is not in its final stage yet. For opponents it would be easy to portray the concept as just another visa scam. The current political climate surrounding this point at present prevents the concept from being discussed seriously. More optimistic participants argued that this concept probably gives room for a more targeted approach (possible advantages: e.g. possibility of testing it on a small scale level and in pilot regions; monitoring the implementation by responsible authorities and evaluating the effects by sound parallel research; complementing rather than replacing existing visa regimes). Therefore, it was argued that the feasibility might be higher than that of the more revolutionary ideas. Anyway, a high degree of public relations input would be needed to advocate this scheme.

The incentives of buying such a visa for relatively high costs (starting at around € 4,000) have been questioned, when one, as a matter of fact, could apply for a tourist visa at a cost of € 15. Tourist visas, however, are not easy to get under the VIS, which currently and, in the future, leaves a substantive amount of people with the option of paying a much higher price to enter Western Europe (i.e. smugglers).

It is furthermore feared that it is unrealistic to regulate the labour markets. Jandl counters this argument by referring to various experiences of the labour markets within the EU that show very different grades of regulation, such as Sweden and Italy. In this context, it was pointed out that the crosscutting responsibilities within governments might also pose some problems. It could, for example, prove difficult to convince the labour market authorities to enforce a higher level of regulation (since they are responsible for work admissions), whereas other sectors like the police (who benefit from reduced smuggling) and the development-policy side (more funds for development aid) stand to gain from it more.

Holger Kolb: 'Pricing Entrance Fee for Migrants'

The concept that is put forward by Holger Kolb is in line with Gary Becker's (1992, 1996) concept of pricing entrance fees for immigrants. According to Kolb, it is a concept that moves away from the current immigration socialism towards a market-economy approach.

Current migration regimes are neither effective nor efficient. Oversized bureaucracy, misallocations and suboptimal service are the results. Furthermore, the increasingly restrictive immigration policies put thousands of willing migrants' lives at risk.

Therefore, Kolb suggests putting a price as an entrance fee on permanent residence permits for European countries. The price would equal the individual costs of the sum of the collective goods consumed, such as streets, security, welfare, etc.

Aside from the price, the criteria for entrance are very few: everyone who can pay the price and is not a terrorist, a criminal nor someone who suffers from contagious diseases can enter the country.

The result of this concept would be increased efficiency and a very small bureaucracy. Migration is to be understood as an investment process. In this light, it can be assumed that the majority of individuals striving for a residence permit in Western countries will be young, rather skilled and ambitious.

It can be argued that this system only allows the solvent migrants to come to Western countries. However, it should be noted, that this is already the case under the current system, as smuggling fees often reach very high sums (e.g. up to $ 45,000 for the US).

Kolb also suggests the introduction of private bank credits for migrants to pay for the entrance fee. In that way, the incentives to migrate legally are even bigger. Irregular migrants who are not able to pay the full price for the journey to the smugglers are often exposed to criminal and violent gangs who act as debt collecting agencies for the smugglers. Having this in mind, the concept is likely to become an instrument to combat human smuggling.

Obviously, this concept is not free of obstacles. Even though the main regulation should be left to the market, the government still needs to implement state guidelines, and the entrance fee has to be set by a political decision.

Another issue is family reunion. Here it can be discussed whether there should be a package price for the whole family, or whether any subsequently following family member should get a price reduction. Further, it should not be neglected that some migrants would only want to stay for a limited amount of time. There must therefore be regulations to pay back some amount of the entrance fee already paid.

As Kolb mentions, the implementation of this concept, in light of the current political discussions, is highly unlikely. Although the right to immigration is not a core right, selling it may be perceived as highly immoral [even though some elements of 'selling' immigration rights for a 'price' of one million euros (or the creation of ten new jobs) are common in current systems as in the 'investor-schemes' in the US or Germany]. Furthermore, politicians and bureaucrats would hardly favour such a concept that in fact curtails their power and budget and would lead to a complete winding up of whole bureaucracies.

Other discussants feared that there will not be a reduction of bureaucracy, but rather a shift of bureaucracy as the labour market would need regulation in order to be held up. Other provocative comments suggested going even so far as to sell the right to have children. This was meant as an indication to where free market policies can lead society. However, Kolb pointed out that contrary to the right to found and to live with a family, there is no universal right to immigration. Market-based solutions in many cases are suspected of being immoral. This also seems to be the case for the proposed entrance fee for immigrants, although, in Kolb's view, nobody would be made worse off compared to the present system.

Notes

1   The views expressed in this article are those of the participants in the workshop only, and not those of ICMPD as a Vienna-based intergovernmental organisation or of its member states.

2   However, it was also pointed out at the workshop that by far the greater majority of 'guestworkers' did not stay, but rather returned.

3   In light of these arguments, the question arises as to what kind of job would be suitable/possible for temporary migrants. It can be argued that these migrants are highly likely to end up with so-called 3D jobs, i.e. the transferring of skills to the country of origin would be doubtful.

List of participants

International Workshop on Innovative Concepts for Alternative Migration Policies

Vienna, 24 and 25 March 2006

IMISCOE workshop organised by: Michael Jandl
International Centre for Migration Policy Development (ICMPD), Vienna

Venue: ICMPD, Gonzagagasse 1, A-1010 Vienna

Participants:
T.J.P. van Os van den Abeelen – ACVZ, The Netherlands
Haleh Chahrokh – ICMPD, Vienna
Jonathan Chaloff – CeSPI, Italy
Jeff Crisp – GCIM/UNHCR, Geneva
Galina Dargova – MoI, Bulgaria
Margarita Delcheva – MoI, Bulgaria
Jeroen Doomernik – IMES, The Netherlands
Franck Düvell – COMPAS Oxford, UK
John Davies – MRC Sussex, UK
Helgo Eberwein – MoI, Austria
Han Entzinger – Erasmus Universiteit, Rotterdam
Michael Jandl – ICMPD, Vienna
Eva Kamaras – MoI, Hungary
Holger Kolb – IMIS, Germany
Judith Kumin – UNHCR, Brussels
Angela Li Rosi – UNHCR at OSCE, Vienna
Jordi García Martínez – DG JLS, European Commission
Rainer Münz – EB, Austria
Christian Schmalzl – MoI, Austria
Nataša Slavíková – MoI, Slovakia
Radoslaw Stryjewski – ORA, Poland and ICMPD, Vienna
Brigitte Suter – ICMPD, Vienna
Theo Veenkamp – DEMOS, UK
Karin Zürcher – BFM, Switzerland

About the authors

Teun van Os van den Abeelen is Coordinating Vice President of the District Court of Amsterdam and Chairman of the Advisory Committee on Aliens Affairs (ACVZ) in The Hague (www.acvz.com).

Jeff Crisp is Special Advisor on Policy Development and Evaluation at UNHCR and the former Director of Policy and Research at the Global Commission on International Migration (www.unhcr.org and www.gcim.org).

Jonathan Chaloff is Senior Researcher at the Centro Studi di Politica Internazionale (CeSPI) in Rome (www.cespi.it).

Haleh Chahrokh is Research Officer at the International Centre for Migration Policy Development (ICMPD) in Vienna (www.icmpd.org).

John Davies is D.Phil. Researcher at the Sussex Centre for Migration Research at the University of Sussex (www.sussex.ac.uk/migration).

Jeroen Doomernik is Senior Researcher at the Institute for Migration and Ethnic Studies (IMES) at the University of Amsterdam (www2.fmg.uva.nl/imes).

Franck Düvell is Senior Researcher at the Centre on Migration, Policy and Society (COMPAS) in Oxford (www.compas.ox.ac.uk).

Michael Jandl is Senior Research Officer at the International Centre for Migration Policy Development (ICMPD) in Vienna (www.icmpd.org).

Holger Kolb is Researcher at the Institute for Migration Research and Intercultural Studies (IMIS) in Osnabrück (www.imis.uni-osnabrueck.de/index.htm).

Judith Kumin is the Regional Representative of the United Nations High Commissioner for Refugees (UNHCR) in Brussels (www.unhcr.org).

Radoslaw Stryjewski is 2006 Jonas Widgren Scholar at the International Centre for Migration Policy Development (ICMPD) in Vienna (www.icmpd.org).

Brigitte Suter is Project Officer at the International Centre for Migration Policy Development (ICMPD) in Vienna (www.icmpd.org).

Theo Veenkamp is Associate Staff Member at the think tank Demos, London (www.demos.co.uk).